RHYMING HISTORY

The Story of England in Verse

RHYMING HISTORY
The Story of England in Verse

by Colin Wakefield

Illustrations by John Partridge

VOLUME FOURTEEN: 1922 – 1939

Depression and the Shadow of War

DHP
Double Honours Publications

RHYMING HISTORY
The Story of England in Verse

VOLUME FOURTEEN: 1922 – 1939
Depression and the Shadow of War

First published in 2022 by Double Honours Publications.

ISBN 978-1-7396882-3-3

Double Honours Publications

Email: info@rhyminghistory.co.uk
Website: www.rhyminghistory.co.uk
Twitter: @Rhyming_History

AUTHOR'S NOTE

This is Volume Fourteen of our *Rhyming History* (still in the writing), which will eventually stretch from Julius Caesar's first arrival in Britain in 55BC to the present day.

Volume Fifteen (The Second World War) will be published in 2023, with subsequent volumes appearing annually. The published volumes are available for sale through our website, Amazon and selected retailers. Volume One (The Romans to the Wars of the Roses) is also available as an ebook through Amazon Kindle. There is a CD of excerpts from Volume One.

These books of verse are intended for those who want to learn more about our history, but in not too solemn a way. I hope they will also appeal to a wider audience, schools, students and historians, and those who simply enjoy reading verse.

John Partridge has again provided witty and entertaining illustrations to accompany the text, for which I am as ever most grateful.

My special thanks are due to Jonathan Dowie for his detailed overview of the text and to Janet Marsten for the creation of our new website. I am also most grateful to Alan Coveney for his expert advice on the text.

Please visit our website for updates on future volumes of the *History* and for news of live performances of the verse.

www.rhyminghistory.co.uk

Colin Wakefield – October 2022

GEORGE THE FIFTH (1910 – 1936)

Three general elections in two years.   **1922**
Unsettled times. There would surely be tears.

The first election: Lloyd George defeated

The Coalition Government fell
In October '22. Just as well,
Cried the Tories. Baldwin and Bonar Law
Led the revolt. Lloyd George, shocked to the core,
Resigned with immediate effect. Sore?
Far from it. 'The Goat' would be back, for sure.
Let the country decide. To widespread surprise,
The British people determined otherwise.

Lloyd George suffered the mother of defeats.
The Tories, true, lost a number of seats,
But the Liberals, down seventy-four,
Were now the smallest party. Labour's score
Increased by eighty-five. The men to blame
Were Lloyd George and Asquith who, to their shame,
Split the Liberal vote. Their old dispute,
Bitter and personal, bore rotten fruit.*

In short, with three hundred and forty-four,
The Tories triumphed. Led by Bonar Law,
They won an overall majority,
Quite unexpected, of over eighty.

---

*They'd fallen out badly during the War.
Lloyd George, unable to take any more,
Had resigned. Poor Asquith, close to collapse,
Was done for. Inevitable? Perhaps.

1

The Labour Party

Winston Churchill lost his seat in Dundee
(A Liberal still). One Clement Attlee
Entered Parliament for the first time.
Ramsay MacDonald, now in his prime,
Was elected Labour leader. His crime,
Many felt, had been to oppose the War.
Newly exonerated on that score,
Would he rise to the challenge? Time would tell.

As proposed by Emanuel Shinwell,
MacDonald looked the perfect candidate.
Shame and ignominy would be his fate
Before the decade was spent. But for now,
MacDonald was setting the pace, and how.
Shinwell had called him "a prince among men".
It was not a matter of 'if', but 'when'
MacDonald would occupy Number Ten.

High ambition indeed! Keir Hardie,
An early hero of the new Party,
First elected in 1892,
Had been one of the first, a select few,
Returned to Parliament for Labour.
In 1906, a year to savour,
Hardie's Independent Labour Party
(ILP) and the so-called LRC
(Labour Representation Committee)
Forged a new political unity
To become the Labour Party. Hardie,
With the support of the secretary
(Ramsay MacDonald) of the LRC,
Saw twenty-nine Labour MPs returned.

These pioneering spirits watched and learned.
While the Liberals got their fingers burned,

The Labour Party made steady progress:
Forty-two MPs elected, no less,
In 1910, and some fifty-seven
In 1918 – hardly, great Heaven,
A breakthrough, but a political *coup*
To leap to one hundred and forty-two
By 1922. Dubbed a 'has-been',
MacDonald had lost his seat in '18,
In Leicester. It had been bound to happen.
Now safely returned for Aberavon,
Where the anti-War faction was strong,
It was clear MacDonald could do no wrong.

The Party was back on song, come what may,
United, determined and here to stay.
Socialism was well on its way.

Bonar Law, a disappointment

The Liberal Party had had its day,
But were Bonar Law's troops fit for the fray?
The picture was mixed, I'm sorry to say.
Austen Chamberlain, hardly a surprise,
Declined to serve. It is fair to surmise
That, as ex-leader, Austen had his pride.
Other Tories, too, were quick to decide
That owing to their former position
As members of the late Coalition
It would be inappropriate to serve.

Law was unfazed. I admire his nerve.
The new Chancellor was Stanley Baldwin –
Relaxed, but in truth as sharp as a pin –
While the temperamental Lord Curzon,
A complex, vain and quarrelsome person,
Stayed in post as Foreign Secretary.
The Cabinet's weakness was plain to see:

Rhyming History

The 'second eleven', Churchill called it.
Neville Chamberlain, to give him credit,
Austen's half-brother, joined the government
As Postmaster General, his intent
To heal the breach between Austen and Law.
Neville failed, alas, and this I deplore.

The sad reality, hard to ignore,   **1923**
Is that Law's new government was a flop.
He may perhaps have been caught on the hop,
Daunted by the prospect of high office.
The Tory campaign bore witness to this,
For Law's election manifesto
Had been lacking in drive, far too narrow.
"The nation's first need," he had declared,
"Is to get on" (I wonder how he dared)

"With its own work." This was to be achieved –
If Bonar Law's words are to be believed –
"With the minimum of interference
"At home" (did you ever hear such nonsense?)
"And of disturbance abroad". Yet he won!

This 'policy', no sooner said than done,
Was put into immediate effect.
His ministers had been led to expect
Non-interference. That is what they got.
An overwhelmingly second-rate lot,
They promised little and delivered less.
When Baldwin, on a trip to the US
To settle the rate at which we should pay
Our debts, agreed, to Bonar Law's dismay,
A higher rate than had been expected,
The Chancellor, able and respected,
Carried the day in Cabinet. Poor Law.
The odds are, he'd have been shown the door
Had Fate not intervened. He had no choice.

The death of Bonar Law

For some months he had been losing his voice,
Then cancer of the throat was diagnosed.
Sooner even than his friends had supposed,
The unfortunate Andrew Bonar Law
Resigned from office. He was sixty-four.
He departed in May, to muted praise,
Having served just two hundred and nine days.
He died in October. Stability?
This Bonar Law managed. Tranquillity?
This he craved – for a politician
A rather singular position.
Did he accomplish it? Who is to say?
He barely had a chance to, anyway.

The BBC

An institution revered today
Is the BBC: a radio play,
News and comment, music, a whole array
Of quiz programmes, light entertainment shows,
Science and the arts, and Lord alone knows
What else... It all began in '22,
When Britain experienced something new:
A national broadcasting service.

The government was thought to prefer this
To the hitherto unregulated
System of 'free' broadcasts. These they hated.
For competing radio frequencies
Were causing considerable unease
In military circles – civil, too.
Interference (this the GPO view)
Put the country's security at risk.
The government's response was bold and brisk.
So was born, out of sheer necessity,
That distinguished body, the BBC.

A business outfit, initially,
Viz. the British Broadcasting Company,
It enjoyed a sort of monopoly.
Earlier broadcasts, in 1920,
By the Wireless Telegraph Company
(Live programmes from Marconi's factory,
In Chelmsford), had proved a splendid success.
The voice of Dame Nellie Melba, no less,
Had moved listeners to tears. The craze
For radio, in those inventive days,
Ran deep and was clearly far from a phase.
The GPO were deluged with requests,
By '22, from vested interests,

For licences – just shy of a hundred.
Hence the decision to form, instead,
One single company (the BBC),
Controlled by one consortium, jointly,
Of leading radio manufacturers.

This new body, as its title infers,
Remained a commercial enterprise.
Effectively a government franchise,
It was financed by a fixed royalty
On all sales (approved by the BBC)
Of wireless receivers. As you can see,
The company enjoyed a monopoly,
But income was driven commercially.

In 1926 a new licence fee
Replaced the idea of a royalty.
The BBC's broadcasting monopoly
Was made more explicit, as the 'Company'
Was transformed into the 'Corporation'.
This radical reorganisation
Was to guarantee the reputation
Of the BBC, across the nation,
For public service. I can tell you for free
That the newly constituted BBC,
Created by Royal Charter, owed its success
To its spirit of independence. I digress…

John Reith (thirty-three) was pleasantly surprised
To see, in the press, a new post advertised:
General Manager of the BBC.
He got the job, and the rest is history.
Reith, it seems, had little or no idea
What broadcasting involved. But they said, "Sign here",
So he did. It was the perfect appointment.
Reith was a dynamo. Wherever he went,

Rhyming History

He commanded trust, respect and loyalty.
His simple mission for the BBC
Was to "inform, educate and entertain",
A policy he stressed again and again.

Reith's influence from the outset was stunning.
He rolled up his sleeves and hit the ground running.
Within days, we are told, of his arrival,
Excerpts from *The Magic Flute* (a revival)
Were aired from Covent Garden. Programmes for schools
Followed in weeks. Never one to suffer fools,
Sir John (as he became) ruled the BBC
With a rod of iron. His drive, energy
And all-embracing code of morality
Were the standard. His announcers set the tone,
Made to wear, as they addressed the microphone,
Dinner jackets! And this was radio, yes!
Rather over the top, I have to confess.

The news headlines, broadcast live from '2LO',
The name of the Marconi House Studio,
Were the first words ever to be heard on air
From the BBC. Listen! You'll feel you're there!

"Marconi House calling!" read Arthur Burrows,
With his 'Oxford' accent. Everyone knows
That this was the only acceptable voice.
Put a plum in your mouth. You had little choice.
The fact that John Reith himself was a Scot
Appeared, in truth, not to matter a lot.

Following the grant, in 1926,
Of the Charter, other programmes joined the mix:
Twickenham (international rugby);
The famous Grand National (from Aintree);
The Boat Race... All now on the BBC.

Trooping the Colour; tennis from Wimbledon;
The first Promenade Concerts… The list goes on.
Even an Orchestra, in 1930,
Joined the payroll: the 'BBC Symphony'.

Radio technique took some getting used to.
Lloyd George and MacDonald (to name but two)
Struggled. Their style of oratory
Was ill suited to the intimacy
Of the microphone and the studio.
Roused to a passion, and in full flow,
Both men could whip up a public meeting
With minimal risk of overheating.
They would carry all before them. Not so,
They soon discovered, on the radio.
Grandiloquent rhetoric? Sadly, no.

This is where Baldwin came into his own,
With his calming voice and cajoling tone.
Honest Stan, best friend of the microphone,
Was warm and relaxed. A fireside chat,
While smoking his pipe and stroking the cat,
Was all that he sought, as simple as that.

The rise of Stanley Baldwin

Following Bonar Law's resignation,
Curzon (ideas above his station)
Expected to be summoned by the King.
Happily, George considered no such thing.
Curzon ("a political jumping Jack,"
Beaverbrook called him) had a certain knack
Of irritating his peers. He was vain,
Pompous, weak and self-satisfied. Insane,
Felt Balfour (one who proffered his advice:
Interference was a cardinal vice),
It would be to foist this arrogant man
On the Tory Party. The quest began.
There was no other choice: Stanley Baldwin.

The candidate's only obvious sin
Was lack of experience: just three years
In the Cabinet. The King, it appears,
Was impressed by Baldwin's simplicity,
His sense of balance and his honesty.
Curzon, bless him, commented frostily
That Baldwin was "nothing, nothing, nothing".
Nonetheless, he was asked to see the King
And invited to form a government.

The opportunity was Heaven-sent,
Though Baldwin's first year, as far as it went,
Proved a fairly dismal disappointment.
Caution was his watchword. Parliament

Was treated to Baldwin's philosophy:
Salvation would come to the country
(Indeed, to the whole world) from "faith, hope, love
"And work" – from these alone. Heavens above!
For Stanley Baldwin, when push came to shove,
Was a simple, homespun man. Or was he?
As for truth, decency and honesty,
It was all an act. Lloyd George got the gist:
"The most formidable antagonist
"Whom I ever encountered." Laid-back, cool,
Calm in a crisis, Baldwin was no fool.
His reputation for indolence
Stanley never shook off. All a pretence?
He would take an age to make up his mind,
But his relaxed attitude, folk would find,
Was a cover. Stability he craved,
And 'strong and stable' was how he behaved.

"A man of the utmost insignificance" –
Curzon again. This of course was nonsense.
A smooth political operator,
Baldwin was certainly no orator,
But he knew what he wanted and he got it,
Even if others were slow to spot it.

The second general election

Yet, within months, he made a grave mistake:
A second election, for pity's sake.
One year into the new Parliament,
Stanley was sufficiently confident
To go to the country. Heaven knows why.
With one's back against the wall, it's worth a try,
Sometimes… But the Tories were riding high:
A majority just short of one hundred.
There was simply no need. Baldwin had blundered.

Rhyming History

Was this to assert his authority?
If so, he squandered his majority.
'Protection' became the key issue –
Well, Baldwin made it so, out of the blue.
The PM bit off more than he could chew.

Unemployment was on the increase, true.
Baldwin committed himself to fight it.
The Tories had been far from united...
Up to now. Baldwin drew them back on side
With his new policy. Time to decide!
A full-blooded election campaign –
With a lot to lose and little to gain –
Was, to the likes of Austen Chamberlain,
A terrific challenge. They backed Baldwin.
Trade tariffs, protection: the sure way
To cut unemployment and win the day.

The Liberal Party (which made a change)
United against them. It may seem strange,
But for once Lloyd George and Asquith agreed
(It wouldn't last) in their bid to succeed.
Labour (under MacDonald) saw no need
For protection, so opposed it too.
Baldwin was ill advised. More than a few
(Curzon included, of course) shared this view.
The King thought the decision unwise,
And tried hard to persuade him otherwise.

The result came as a nasty surprise.
December the 6th, the date of the poll,
Was a government nightmare. Heads would roll
(Or would they?). In terms of total votes cast,
There was little movement. The Libs came last,
While gaining 200,000 votes more
Than in '22, just a year before;
In strong second place, and hard to ignore,

Were Labour: 100,000 votes more.
The Tories topped the poll, though with a score
200,000 less. This modest amount,
However, after taking into account
The voting system, where votes alone don't count,
Proved oddly decisive. The Tories were toast.
For under the infamous 'first past the post',
It's the dispersal of votes that matters most,
Between the parties. Liberals and Labour
Gained ninety seats between them, the true flavour
Of an uneven system. The Tories lost
Roughly the same number and found, to their cost,
That they had forfeited their majority.
The government lost all its authority.

Baldwin bows out

Labour gained fifty seats and retained their place
As the second largest party. With good grace,
Or perhaps, as some suggested, to save face,
The PM decided not to go quite yet.
He bided his time until the Commons met
And, on the 21st of January,
1924, as was customary,   **1924**
Resigned after a vote of no confidence.

The King resolved to give Labour "a fair chance".
A curious little political dance,
On and off, had been taking place in the wings.
A new alliance, of all unlikely things,
A Liberal-Tory pact, under Asquith,
Was proposed in Labour's stead. I mean, as if.
Or the Tories should throw out Stanley Baldwin
And replace him with Balfour, or Chamberlain –
Not Neville, but their former leader, Austen.
For the prospect of a Labour government
Had thrown the die-hards into a ferment.

One organ to predict chaos, without fail,
Was the ever-dependable *Daily Mail*.
The City of London voiced growing alarm
At the financial outlook. Massive harm,
It foresaw, to the British economy.

The first Labour Prime Minister

Wiser counsels prevailed. Best to wait and see.
The only proper course, politically,
As the King, Baldwin and Asquith could agree,
Was to end the perilous uncertainty
And let Labour loose to govern. Probably,
The pundits prophesied, it would end in tears.
Within a matter of months, rather than years,
Baldwin would be back. As far as he could see,
Labour in government, a minority,
Could do little or nothing to rock the boat.
The Liberals would keep MacDonald afloat,
For a while. Stanley, never a man to gloat,
Would bide his time. When the expected day came
For Labour's downfall, he'd re-assert his claim,
And the pesky Liberals would bear the blame.

This was Baldwin's strategy, at any rate:
Let Labour have its head, then sit back and wait.
MacDonald, for his part, did not hesitate.
To accept office without power, some said,
Was a folly. At this MacDonald saw red.
It was the Party's responsibility
To take up the challenge. A minority?
Pah! Labour was fit and would rise to the test.
MacDonald, Prime Minister, would do his best.

King George the Fifth wrote this in his Diary
For the 22nd of January:
"Today 23 years ago" (precisely)

"Dear Grandmama died. I wonder what
"She would have thought" (I think not a lot)
"Of a Labour Government!" MacDonald
Had first to be sworn in, so we are told,
As Privy Councillor. He accepted
The great office of state, as expected,
Of Prime Minister. The King, his new boss,
Recommended he hire, from Moss Bros.,
Any item of Court dress he might need.

This point MacDonald was quick to concede,
With gratitude. Others were not so keen.
Such blatant flim-flammery was obscene –
This from some of his ministers (working class).
Ceremonial dress? A pain in the arse.

MacDonald's government

Yet governing Britain was hardly a farce.
Labour was in office by permission
Of the people, and MacDonald's mission
Was to prove himself worthy. Stability,
Confidence, fiscal responsibility
And competence would earn the nation's trust.
A strong, realistic programme was a must.

He failed, though he scored some successes – just.
His Chancellor, Snowden, balanced the books,
Proving that Labour, far from being crooks,
Could manage the budget responsibly.
MacDonald's Health Minister, John Wheatley,
Confounded Labour's critics completely
With his hugely popular Housing Act.
Homes for rent (an unpalatable fact)
Were scarce and in high demand. Wheatley increased
The subsidy (on new rental builds, at least)
To councils. His was a long-term strategy,
A fifteen-year plan. The building industry,
The government and local authorities
Worked together, with the help of subsidies,
To build over half a million houses.

The kind of bitterness that this arouses,
And envy, is of interest. John Wheatley,
A figure of outstanding ability,
Along with his 'Clydeside credibility'
As a highly regarded Glasgow MP,
May have fuelled a rare sense of jealousy
In MacDonald. For there was no place for him
In Mac's second government. Signally dim.

There was progress in education too.
Concrete achievements were relatively few,

Owing to the brief life of the government.
But Labour's policies were a testament
To its high ideals and thirst for reform.

Strict economies for schools had been the norm
Under the Tories and the Coalition.
Happily, Labour reversed the position.
C. P. Trevelyan, at Education,
Showed skill in his dogged determination
To raise standards in schools across the nation.

He reviewed many of the economies
Imposed by the mean, penny-pinching Tories.
Local education authorities
Were afforded greater independent scope,
And Trevelyan even proposed (some hope!)
Raising the school leaving age to fifteen.

The Second World War was to intervene
Before this could be achieved. Nevertheless,
Trevelyan, in his short time in harness,
Displayed a far-sightedness and a goodwill
That should serve as an example to us still.

Foreign affairs

MacDonald, his own Foreign Secretary,
Mastered a new style of diplomacy,
Both relaxed and profitable. Germany
Had been badly served, economically,
By the harsh terms of the Versailles Treaty,
To which she had not even been a party.

The French had occupied the Ruhr Valley
In a vain attempt to enforce the payment
Of reparations. France, the main claimant,

Was stubborn in her demands, while Germany,
On her knees, as everybody could see,
Had not the faintest chance of paying the bill.

MacDonald conducted himself with great skill.
Unemployment was an ever-present ill,
At home and abroad. What to do about it?

There'd be no recovery (who could doubt it?)
Without a resurgence in Britain's exports.
While continental Europe was out of sorts
(A euphemism, this), there was no prospect,
Should the decline in foreign trade go unchecked,
Of advancement on the domestic front. So,
It was Mac's mission to let the French know,
In no uncertain terms, that they should withdraw,
Without further delay, their troops from the Ruhr,
And enter into negotiations
For a review of the reparations
That Germany should be made to pay. Well,
MacDonald played a blinder, truth to tell.

MacDonald's diplomatic skill

He brought the Germans and French together,
In London, in July. Stormy weather?
Not so. Doubt and mistrust were swept away,
As Germany's capacity to pay
Was considered at last. Cynicism
And contempt gave way to realism.

The French, not exempt from criticism,
Nonetheless, for the first time since the War,
Lowered their guard. Withdrawal from the Ruhr
Was a most unpopular move, for sure,
Among hard-liners. To level the score,

Depression and the Shadow of War

I'm glad to say, Anglo-French relations
Took an upward turn. The League of Nations,
In a fresh round of negotiations,
Was perceived to provide a sound guarantee
For peace, through disarmament, security
And arbitration – the bedrock, all three,
For the 'absence of war'. For the French, clearly,
Were fearful that a powerful Germany
Would threaten her borders, as she had before.
The hideous memory of the Great War
Loomed large in the French psyche, bitter and raw.

German reparations took a back seat,
However, for the next five years. Quite a feat.
All down to MacDonald, his triumph complete.

He enjoyed considerably less success
With Soviet Russia, I must confess.
Mac seriously upset the right-wing press
With his decision, in February,
To give recognition to that country.
The poor PM was up another gum tree
When he guaranteed a commercial loan
To the Soviets (the idea his own),
As part of a more intricate arrangement
For the staggered, long-overdue repayment
Of Russia's pre-Revolution debts.

Bolshevism! The mother of all threats!
The mere whiff of Soviet sympathies
Was a gift to MacDonald's enemies –
For Labour, the worst of horror stories.
Liberals were livid, make no mistake.
Lloyd George dubbed the Russian loan "a fake".
He scented blood. The Prime Minister's fall
Was imminent, to the delight of all.

The fall of the Labour government

What brought Labour down? It was a close call.
For the cause, when it came, was trivial.
A leading Communist, J. R. Campbell,
Was charged with incitement to mutiny,
For calling for a 'don't shoot' policy
In the left-wing paper, *Workers' Weekly*.
Soldiers were urged not to open fire
On fellow workers, rather to retire
To barracks. Academic, anyway:
For there was no current risk of affray,
Riot or civil disobedience.
The charge was dropped by Labour. This made sense.
'Incitement' was a very old offence.
An Act of 1797
Had been called in aid, merciful Heaven!
The prosecution was plain nonsense.

Was this political interference?
Yes, screamed the Tories! The course of justice
Had been tampered with. It had come to this:
Ramsay MacDonald siding with the Trots!
The Liberals recommended (the clots)
A House of Commons select committee.
Sick of being in a minority,
Labour poured scorn on Asquith's compromise.
Baldwin supported it, to some surprise,
Leading the Prime Minister (was this wise?)
To make it an issue of confidence.
Had he simply had enough? He was dense
If he reckoned he could possibly win.

Honesty, MacDonald's besetting sin,
Was his own undoing. He bore the cost
Of his integrity. Of course, he lost –

By one hundred and seventy-three votes.
All Labour men (I hope you're taking notes),
All one hundred and ninety-one of them,
Backed MacDonald to the hilt. No problem.

A third general election

So, the country went to the polls again,
Plunged into an election campaign
For the third time in the course of two years.
King George was reluctant, so it appears,
To grant another dissolution –
But this was the only solution,
According to Asquith and Baldwin, both,
When consulted. Baldwin was nothing loth,
Of course, to have another poll so soon.
This was the Tories' golden afternoon.

The Liberals were squeezed: one hundred seats down,
As even their leader was drummed out of town.
Asquith lost to the Labour man at Paisley,
Having fought a half-hearted campaign, lazy
And uninspiring. Herbert became a Lord,
Choosing the defunct title, Earl of Oxford.
Lloyd George hung on in Caernarvon. The Libs won,
However, just forty seats. Their day was done.

The return of Baldwin

Baldwin's Tories were already on a roll,
When publication, days before the poll,
Of a fake letter threatened to take its toll
On Labour's prospects. Trumpeted in *The Times*,
The 'Zinoviev letter' hinted at crimes
To be incited by British Communists,
Unashamed and unreserved apologists

For their much-admired comrades in Moscow.
The Times was eager for its readers to know
Of Russian Communist links with Labour.

The letter 'revealed', to give you a flavour,
The closeness of the Ruskies to the Party
And to its leaders. MacDonald was "tardy"
(*The Times*) in his dismissal of the letter.
There's little doubt he could have done better.
Publication had caused a perfect storm:
MacDonald's response was at best lukewarm.

Be that as it may, the Labour vote increased
By one million, a testament, at least,
To the common sense of the electorate.
In terms simply of seats, Labour dropped a bit
(Down by forty-two), but the main benefit
Was reaped by the Tories – predicted, perhaps,
By canny Stanley. The Liberal collapse
Had been Baldwin's strategy all along.
The new Prime Minister was well on song:
Over four hundred seats. He could do no wrong.

Lilian Baylis and the Old Vic

The 1920s were happily the time
When Lilian Baylis was in her prime,
Manager of the glorious Old Vic.
Enterprising, dogged and heroic,
Baylis was a one-off. She brought Shakespeare
To the poorer classes. A pioneer,
She lived for the Vic, and she knew no fear.

She began her unusual career
Out in South Africa, where her family
Had emigrated. Trained, initially,

Depression and the Shadow of War

As a dancer and a violinist,
The Gipsy Revellers (not to be missed)
Was the name of her parents' touring act,
A small song-and-dance troupe, to be exact.
Performance skills Lilian never lacked,
Talents put to good use, in later years,
In raising money, from paupers and peers,
From rich and poor, for her precious Vic.

Her ways were blunt and unbureaucratic,
Some say chaotic; the rows, volcanic.
She worked all hours, a one-woman team,
Seven days a week, to fulfil her dream:
Theatre for the people. Her success
Sprang from her vision, no more, no less,
Of the arts for all, as a human right.
This Baylis delivered, night after night.

She returned to England, aged twenty-four,
In 1898. The Boer War
Was soon to begin. The young Lilian
Was content now to settle in London,
As assistant to her mother's sister,
Her aunt, Emma Cons. She had missed her,
Remembering how she had held on tight
To her seat, there on the very first night
(At the age of six) of the Cons era.
She ran the Victoria Theatre
(The 'Old Vic') as a temperance venue.

For an entertainment hall this was new.
In that part of London there was no place
For a good night out (a perfect disgrace,
To the mind of Miss Cons, a Christian)
Where honest families could have some fun,
Free from the curse of the demon drink.
Emma determined to sever the link

Rhyming History

Between places of leisure and the booze.
A temperance hall was wonderful news:
A full, mixed programme would banish the blues.
People flocked to the Vic. Concerts, revues,
Opera, military bands they got –
Cinema (later), recitals, the lot.
No drama, interestingly enough:
Too highbrow, perhaps? The standard was rough,
But the Vic would play to thousands a night.
Emma must have been doing something right.

When Lilian Baylis was thirty-eight,
Emma Cons died. She had asked her aunt straight:
"What about the Vic, Emmie?" Her reply?
"You are there, dear." It is hard to deny
That this was a turning point. It made sense
To apply for a theatre licence.
This Lilian did. People's theatre,
The Vic's new owner resolved, and Shakespeare
Were not incompatible. The first year
(1914) was not a success. This,
It seems, was not the fault of Miss Baylis,
But the policy, rather hit and miss,
Of Rosina Filippi, an actress,
Who staged two plays, *The Merchant of Venice*
And *Romeo and Juliet.* She failed.
She lost money. The project was derailed,
And poor Miss Filippi, out of her ear,
Was heard of no more. The draw of Shakespeare,
However, was stronger. Under Ben Greet,
Actor-manager, the Vic found its feet.

The great Greet worked for Lilian Baylis
For four years. Paid only his expenses,
And at first, I believe, not even those,
His secret lay in the programme he chose:

The more popular plays, the *Othello*'s,
The *Macbeth*'s, which, as everyone knows,
Pull in the crowds. From October '14
To April '15, Ben Greet staged sixteen
(Yes, sixteen) Shakespeare plays, I kid you not.

You'll appreciate, that's rather a lot.
You may be further impressed when you hear,
Apart from the mass staging of Shakespeare,
That the Vic presented operas too:
Seventeen in six months (more than a few) –
Rigoletto and *Faust*, to name but two.
Shakespeare was staged on Mondays and Wednesdays;
Opera on Thursdays and Saturdays;
Illustrated lectures were on Tuesdays –

Rhyming History

A schedule calculated to amaze.
I'm not quite sure what happened on Fridays.

School parties were welcome at matinées,
"On special terms". Prices were kept low
For children and families, who could go,
For tuppence or less, to the gallery.
This was Lilian's top priority:
She couldn't afford to let them in free –
The Old Vic was never a charity –
But access to drama of quality,
For the poorest patrons, that was the key.

The strictest rigours of economy
Were practised by Miss Baylis. As late,
It appears, as 1928,
A production's entire budget
(Excluding wages), for costumes and set,
Was thirty-eight pounds. The standard, you bet,
Was rough and ready. Yet nobody cared:
While the crew and stage directors despaired,
Costume designers and actors to boot,
The general public gave not a hoot.
Affordable seats and a great night out:
A winning ticket, no shadow of doubt.
Half-price admission became the norm
For "His Majesty's Forces in Uniform".

The Vic was lacking in facilities.
There was no running water, if you please,
Bar a single tap located stage left
(On the prompt side). The players were bereft:
No dressing rooms, no proper box office,
No wardrobe and no scene dock. Miss Baylis
Occupied a box for her office. This,
During shows, is where she cooked sausages.

As for actors' wages, you want to weep.
"Send me a good actor, but send him cheap,"
She would pray to God. But the actors came!

Even Laurence Olivier, his fame
As a Hollywood star the guarantee
Of a huge following, gave up his fee
Of five hundred pounds a week, in movies,
For twenty-five at the Vic. Salaries?
Pah! It was acting opportunities,
Above all, that counted. Olivier
Never regretted, to his dying day,
His season at the Vic (Lilian's last:
1937). Larry learned fast:
An athletic Hamlet, a fine Iago
(Opposite Ralph Richardson's Othello),

Rhyming History

And Coriolanus. He learned the ropes
As a classical actor. His high hopes
Were well rewarded. Thirty years later,
Britain's new National 'The-atre',
Led by Olivier as director,
After an early start at Chichester,
Took up residence at the Vic. That's Fate –
In my opinion, at any rate.

To return to the early days, Ben Greet
Had an eagle eye for talent. One treat
Was the young Ernest Milton as Hamlet.
Baylis was pleased: "You have the face for it,"
She said. So Milton's career began
As the Old Vic's popular leading man.

As the theatre's reputation grew,
Its distinguished players, to name a few,
Included Gielgud (first as a walk-on)
And, in the thirties, even Charles Laughton –
As Angelo in *Measure for Measure*,
A triumph, allegedly, to treasure,
Though he failed as Macbeth, the acid test.
"Never mind, dear, I'm sure you did your best."
Praise from Miss Baylis? Well, don't hold your breath!
"One day you may be quite a good Macbeth."

Most of the leading actors of the day,
Edith Evans, Balliol Holloway,
Peggy Ashcroft and Judith Anderson,
Appeared at the Old Vic. Ralph Richardson,
Donald Wolfit even, Flora Robson,
The great Martita Hunt… The list goes on.

The directors, however, set the pace.
Greet lasted four years, far from a disgrace,

Depression and the Shadow of War

With all the bombing raids during the war.
Sybil Thorndike arrived at the stage door,
Late one night, having dodged the Zeppelins.
Lilian was waiting. Who cared two pins
For the pesky Germans? She'd missed her call.
Zeppelin raids hardly mattered at all.

A former member of the company,
Robert Atkins, having served his country,
Returned to the Vic. Destined to go far,
He added to the Shakespeare repertoire
Such lesser known plays as *Troilus*
And Cressida, Titus Andronicus

Rhyming History

And *Timon of Athens.* For seven years
He endured the tantrums, temper and tears
Of Miss Baylis, and raised standards all round.
His eye was sharp and his judgement was sound.
Atkins was succeeded by Andrew Leigh,
Then Harcourt Williams and, finally,
By the legendary Tyrone Guthrie.

Now Lilian Baylis, it seems to me,
Given her faults, was extremely lucky
In her choice of directors. Quality,
In the face of constant adversity,
Was never compromised to stay afloat.
She had a favourite saying (I quote):
"Monday nights have got to be better."
This she observed to the very letter.

Although she lurched from crisis to crisis,
Financially, Lilian Baylis
Persisted in the craziest of dreams.
By now the Vic was bursting at the seams.
She needed another theatre. Yes –
This was the height of midsummer madness.
She wished to start a dance company too.
With such wild fantasies, what do you do?

You press on! Never one to hesitate,
She contrived to raise funds to renovate
The site of Sadler's Wells, in Islington.
Opera? Dance? No sooner said, than done.

Running a ballet school in Kensington
Was Ninette de Valois. The young Ninette
Approached Baylis. For a pittance (you bet:
One pound a week), Lilian took her on
To teach the actresses movement. She shone!

Depression and the Shadow of War

Miss Baylis was concerned, one understands,
That no one knew what to do with their hands.
Miss de Valois was also paid two pounds –
A fee to treasure, the figure astounds –
To arrange any choreography
Required for the Shakespeare repertory.

This was in 1926. Ninette
Was in clover. She had heard nothing yet.
At Sadler's Wells a ballet company
Was planned by Miss Baylis and it was she,
Ninette de Valois, who was given charge.
Now this was opportunity writ large.
The new venue opened in '31.
A ballet company was born. Deal done.

The most famous names in British ballet,
Toasted and celebrated to this day,
Started at the Wells: Frederick Ashton
(Choreographer) and Robert Helpmann;
Anton Dolin; the young Margot Fonteyn
(Born Peggy Hookham, but that was insane);
And, leading the company from day one,
Alicia Markova. It was fun.
It was hard graft. It was a huge success.

How Baylis did it is anyone's guess.
Mark her legacy: the Royal Ballet;
The National Theatre (Olivier
Made it happen, but in her own sweet way
Lilian sowed the seeds, and good for her);
The English National Opera;
The Royal Ballet School… No subsidy,
No government funding: nothing for free.
But Baylis became the true champion
Of the right to art. Thank you, Lilian.

Baldwin's triumph

In the Tory landslide of '24,
Asquith's Liberals were shown the door –
MacDonald lost forty-two seats to boot.
Stanley Baldwin's triumph was absolute.
Within eleven months of his defeat,
In '23, he was back on his feet.
The knives had been out, but Baldwin survived.
He kept his cool and the Party revived.

He played a blinder. A man of some wealth,
All he could offer, he claimed, was himself:
"I never sought office." All said and done,
Stanley was a plain, simple Englishman.
"The sound of a scythe against a whetstone" –
The very soul of England! This alone,
He pledged, it was his duty to preserve.
As "one of yourselves" he promised to serve.
We choose, I suppose, the men we deserve.

Domestic affairs

To be fair, the Tory manifesto
(As we'd call it today) struck a strong blow
For progress and modernisation.
Baldwin proposed new legislation
To extend national insurance,
Pensions and (this made perfect good sense)
Health benefits for those in employment.
An overhaul of local government
Was also a promise. This was achieved,
If the books I've read are to be believed,
In one Parliament. Don't be deceived:
A huge programme of social reform
Was on offer – from Tories, hardly the norm.

The strength of Neville Chamberlain

This was the brief of Neville Chamberlain.
A private man, and as unlike Baldwin
As chalk to cheese, he was misunderstood
On a grand scale. For Chamberlain was good,
Upright and hard-working. He eschewed fame.
Munich apart, he would have made his name
As an outstanding inter-war figure.

He attracted more than the odd snigger,
Lacking humour (on the surface, at least)
And human warmth. Success, that fickle beast,
Came to him late. Nearly fifty years old
When he entered the House, Neville was cold,

Rhyming History

Austere and forbidding. Even his dress –
Not without reason, I have to confess –
Was a joke, Edwardian and prim:
Hence 'the Coroner', as some called him.

Macmillan (who liked him, one of the few)
Thought him "very, very narrow in view",
But "a nice man". Lloyd George, it would appear,
Detested him, regarding him, we hear,
As "a good mayor of Birmingham…" (I fear,
Alas, a sting in the tail) "…in an off year".

Over the course of Baldwin's government,
Twenty-one Acts (a glowing testament
To Neville Chamberlain's resolve) were passed,
Of twenty-five proposed. Folk were aghast
(Including Labour) with admiration.
For this was social legislation:
Housing, pensions, health, local affairs.

The PM had been taken unawares
By honest Neville turning down the post
Of Chancellor. What mattered to him most
Was welfare. That was the true gist of it.
He could make a far better fist of it
As Minister of Health, and so it proved.
Neville made his choice, and Baldwin approved.

His half-brother, Austen (a surprise, this),
Agreed to take on the Foreign Office.
As an ex-Tory leader, he'd refused –
Having felt, I suggest, sore and ill-used –
A job in Baldwin's former government.
All that was now forgotten. The present
Was what counted most. The past was the past.
Baldwin's new Cabinet was built to last.

The return of Churchill

Events unfolded remarkably fast.
The unpredictable Winston Churchill,
After twenty years a good Liberal,
Had returned to the Tory fold. Baldwin
Snapped him up. Winston took it on the chin,
When offered the Chancellorship. He thought,
Bless him (and was not a little distraught),
Baldwin had meant that unappealing post,
The Duchy of Lancaster. He'd hoped, most,
For the Admiralty and was surprised,
To put it mildly, when he realised
That Baldwin meant the Exchequer! Funny,
If it hadn't been so sad… For money
Had never been Winston Churchill's strong point.
Eager, as ever, not to disappoint,
He accepted the offer with good grace.

His colleagues were horrified. To save face, **1925**
And to satisfy the Tory old guard,
Men from the pre-War world, he swallowed hard,
And in his first Budget, in '25,
Churchill announced a return (saints alive!)
To the Gold Standard. Since 1919,
Gold had been held in suspension. Keen,
I imagine, to raise Britain's profile
And to start his Chancellorship in style,
Churchill embarked on this dangerous move
With misplaced confidence. It was to prove,
At best, a flop; at worst, a disaster.
British exports fell faster and faster,
Having been in decline for many years.

The pound was overvalued, stoking fears
Among economists, who had no doubt
That Britain was in for a trading 'drought':

Exports were quite simply too expensive.
The harm done was costly and extensive.
From a high point in 1924,
British exports decreased (this I deplore)
By almost a third in the next six years.

In 1931 (yes, there were tears),
Gold was abandoned. Churchill, it appears,
Had made a big mistake. Thank you, Winston.
He never acknowledged the damage done.
Politics, to him, were all rather fun.

The Locarno Pact

Neville Chamberlain's half-brother, Austen,
With the full support of Stanley Baldwin,
Negotiated the Locarno Pact,
Signed in December. Now, it's a sad fact
That this non-aggression treaty,
Designed to offer a guarantee
Of European security,
Did nothing of the kind. Italy,
And Great Britain, stood as guarantors
To stop the outbreak of future wars
Between Belgium, France and Germany.

It also included a guarantee
Of the Franco-German border. To me,
This appears eminently sensible.
What, however, was reprehensible
Is that nothing was ever put in place
To implement it. A perfect disgrace.

There was little more cynical than this.
The Pact was built on the empty promise
Of military support. Some premise!
Britain made no effort, I think you'll find,
To prepare for anything of the kind.

Regrettably, the great Locarno Pact
Was simple verbiage, in the abstract,
Against aggression. For what it lacked
Were teeth. One thing good did come out of it:
Germany, at last, was considered fit
To enrol as a member (about time)
Of the League of Nations. In his prime,
The Foreign Secretary, much lauded
For his efforts, was roundly applauded.

Chamberlain, a thoroughly decent bloke,
Achieved what he did with mirrors and smoke.
Despite the Pact being a non-starter,
Austen was made a Knight of the Garter.

Baldwin's style of government

Baldwin preferred accommodation
To any sort of confrontation.
To give you a taste of this, a flavour,
He forged good relations with Labour.
Warm-hearted, relaxed, even jocular,
He took pains to make himself popular
With all sides of the House. You may well scoff,
But this inspired strategy paid off,
In spades, in the dark days of '31,
When Baldwin emerged as the only one
With the gravitas to save the country.

Labour, up the proverbial gum tree,
Deserted MacDonald. Out on a limb,
He turned to Baldwin. It was down to him.
At the time it strained credibility,
But Stanley's tact, proven ability
And calm demeanour ensured stability.

Industrial relations

All that's for later. British industry
Was in a pickle. Though, admittedly,
The number of strikes, in terms of days lost,
Declined in '25, the total cost
Was nonetheless high: eight million days –
A figure calculated to amaze –
Involving some half a million men,
In six hundred different disputes. When,

Depression and the Shadow of War

Asked Baldwin, would relations improve?
The government should stay at one remove
(So he believed), and the Cabinet too,
But wasn't there anything they could do?

Then came the perfect opportunity
To declare his hand. A backbench Tory,
David Macquisten (ever heard of him?
I doubt it; he was singularly dim)
Proposed making the political levy
Paid by union members voluntary,
Rather than (as was current) compulsory.
Labour would lose a large chunk of their income –
A welcome result, according to some,
But in Baldwin's view decidedly dumb.

On March the 6th, 1925,
The PM went into overdrive.
The best speech of his political life
Baldwin delivered. Industrial strife
He abhorred, and political schism.

Risking heavy backbench criticism,
He weighed in. With his massive majority,
He could stamp his personal authority
On David Macquisten's proposed measure.

But Baldwin preferred to "make a gesture
"To the country". He resolved to create
"A new atmosphere", and stretch the debate
Above and beyond party politics.
This was no time for idle heroics:
"We are not going to fire the first shot."
Whether Tory die-hards liked it or not,
"We stand for peace". He recalled, looking back,
His family firm. No one got the sack.

Rhyming History

Old men smoked their pipes with impunity:
"Not an inefficient community."
Baldwin appealed, above all, for unity.

In short, the PM went in for the kill,
And that was the end of Macquisten's Bill.
Stanley concluded (this he could well afford)
With a prayer: "Give peace on our time, O Lord!"

His speech galvanised the Commons. Sadly,
For a significant majority,
His words had the whiff of complacency.
And as for industrial harmony,
For better or worse, it was not to be.

The miners

Discontent in the mining industry
Had reached a new high. The obduracy,
Of the owners, had alienated
The mineworkers. The pits were outdated,
And dangerous. Modernisation
They scorned, to the intense frustration
Of both the Miners' Federation
And the government. Nationalisation,
A dirty word, had been kicked into touch.
Neither party felt inclined (well, not much)
To engage in talks. Coalfields in the Ruhr,
Back in production since '24,
Had knocked the bottom out of British coal.
The German industry was on a roll.

Mines were running at a loss. What to do?
To tell the honest truth, nobody knew.
Putting the pits into profit again
Would involve the miners taking the strain,
So argued the owners. That kind of pain,

Countered the workers, was not on the cards.
They sent the employers their best regards,
But their message was plain. To take a cut
In wages? Sorry, mate: anything but.

The owners insisted on longer hours
And lower earnings. Nobody had powers,
Least of all the government, to enforce
An agreement. The TUC (what sauce,
Huffed the owners) sought to negotiate –
But no, the miners were left to their fate.

Their slogan, "Not a penny off the pay"
Touched a nerve – "Not a minute on the day".

The owners dug in. German mining boomed,
On the Ruhr, while here a miners' strike loomed.
The transport workers and the railwaymen
Backed the mineworkers. It was only then
That the government took proper notice.

The TUC (Baldwin took note of this)
Gave orders for a total embargo
On the movement of coal, a severe blow
To hopes of a constructive settlement.

This, of course, they would only implement
In the event of a strike. In his heart,
Baldwin believed (an unpromising start)
That a wage cut was inevitable.
But extra hours? That seemed terrible.

Deadlock. The owners threatened a lockout.
A general strike, no shadow of doubt,
Was now in prospect. With hours to go –
A mere twenty-six, if you want to know –

Baldwin stepped in. He'd said that he wouldn't.
But sit on his hands? He simply couldn't.
His answer was a fudge, it seems to me:
The payment to the mining industry
Of a large sum of government money,
In the form of a 'bridging' subsidy,
To buy time for a public inquiry
To report on the subject of mining.

Every cloud has a silver lining…
Well, not this one. The Samuel Report
Died the death. A solution was sought,
But none was found. The Report was a farce,
All three hundred pages of it. 'Long grass'
And 'kicked into' are words that spring to mind –
Or am I being unduly unkind?

I don't think so. Samuel solved nothing.   **1926**
Reorganisation was one thing.
This was floated, but rejected point blank
By the owners. The Report, to be frank,
Was a wash-out. Amalgamation
Of small pits, a recommendation
For more pit head baths, even holidays
(Believe it or not) with pay, were ways,
For miners, of sugaring the pill.

But such proposals were run-of-the-mill,
Compared to the price the workers would pay:
Lower wages. A moot point, anyway.
For the employers refused to give way
On any of the 'improvements' proposed.
The miners were vehemently opposed
To a pay cut. A longer working day
Samuel rejected, I'm pleased to say –
But wages must be cut without delay.

The General Strike

Both parties were loth to negotiate.
Samuel offered too little, too late,
And the PM refused to mediate.
A general strike, now a certainty,
Was promptly endorsed by the TUC,
Who assumed full responsibility
For the strike. Their support (and sympathy)
For the miners' cause was solid and strong –
But they made it up as they went along.
In the end it all went horribly wrong.

The Tory government was well on song.
Detailed preparations had been made
For a strike, which of course had been delayed
By Samuel. The PM was dismayed,
Nonetheless, at the progress of events,
Appalled, as were other men of good sense.
His best efforts for peace had been derailed.
As he readily confessed: "I have failed."

The action began on May the 3rd.
Winston Churchill called the strikers (absurd,
If not so ignorant) "the enemy".
King George condemned this as inflammatory.
These were his subjects. In an emergency
Both sides deserved respect, for Heaven's sake.
The government would make "a grave mistake"
To deprive the unions of funds: wise,
Humane and, coming from George, no surprise.

The TUC were interested, too,
In lowering the temperature. Phew!
They only called the big unions out,
At first – the ones with the maximum clout:

Rhyming History

The transport workers and the railwaymen,
The builders... Even so, eight out of ten
Of those employed in heavy industry,
Including gas and electricity,
Downed tools. The smaller unions were kept,
As it were, in reserve. The miners wept,
When after just nine days the TUC
Called off the general strike. Now, to me,
It's clear they never had a strategy.

How did this come to pass? Well, for a start,
Good old England refused to fall apart.

Though some areas witnessed violence,
Instances were rare. Most people saw sense.
Those carried away in the excitement,
And charged with violence or incitement,
Numbered under four thousand – not a lot,
Given that the strikers, like it or not,
Were in their millions. No one was shot;
Nobody died. One isolated case
Was reported (an absolute disgrace)
Of a wicked attempt to sabotage
A railway line. However, by and large,
The strike was more peaceful than expected,
With rights on both sides duly respected.
The country muddled along. Food supplies –
A stark fact that few today realise –
Were uninterrupted. Churchill, the fool,
Not one to pull his punches, as a rule,
Despatched twenty armoured cars to Hyde Park
From the Docks (what was this, some kind of lark?)
To escort a consignment of flour.

Winston, hardly the man of the hour,
Thwarted in his attempts to cause a scare,
Was laughed out of court. He was all hot air.

Plymouth police caused Baldwin some distress,
By playing football with the strikers! Yes,
This at the instigation, no less,
Of the Chief Constable. I say Baldwin,
But... Though this was a fight he had to win –
He viewed the strike as a direct attack
On the constitution – he had a knack
Of sitting on the fence. He saw, perhaps,
The Plymouth cops as thoroughly good chaps.
For the strike was the mother of mishaps,
And anything done to defuse it...
Well, who was Baldwin to refuse it?

For some, the strike was a bit of a laugh.
The toffs? They would show the strikers, not half!
The dockers sent them for an early bath,
As volunteers succumbed to fatigue.
Unloading cargo was out of their league.

Rhyming History

Undergrads from the universities,
Down from Oxford and Cambridge, if you please,
Drove buses and (what a terrific wheeze!)
Directed traffic: a bit of a breeze,
With fortunately no fatalities.
Massed ranks of volunteers (most of these
Men and women of the middle classes)
Kept Britain working. The silly arses
Were in the minority. This was war,
Of a sort, a direct challenge to the law.
Gas and electric plants were kept going,
By naval ratings. There was no knowing,
However, how long Britain's luck would last.
If the mood turned sour, it could run out fast.

The PM made a radio broadcast,
On the 8th of May, on the BBC.
His tone was firm, but conciliatory.
Baldwin denied, unequivocally,
That he wanted anything but justice
For the miners. But he emphasised this:
The general strike was a clear assault
On the whole community. Call a halt,
And honest Stanley gave his guarantee
That the miners would be treated fairly.
He refused to surrender the safety
Or, as he put it, "the security
"Of the British Constitution". No,
There were no lengths to which he would not go
To reach a just settlement: "a square deal
"For miners and owners." Was this man real?

His broadcast, it seems, was the catalyst
The TUC needed. Here is the gist:
Samuel intervened. The compromise
He proposed (which came as little surprise)

Depression and the Shadow of War

Was that once 'reorganisation'
Was agreed (the recommendation
In his Report), then a new Wages Board
Would assess what the owners could afford,
With pay cuts mooted only at that stage.
His proposals caused absolute outrage
Among miners. There were no guarantees
That recommendations such as these
(For improvements) would be acceptable
To the owners. It was contemptible,
After what had already taken place,
Even to talk of wage cuts. A disgrace.

Nonetheless, as a way of saving face,
The TUC, with a sigh of relief,
Leapt at Samuel's proposals. Good grief!
The miners, who weren't even consulted,
Were apoplectic. Ignored, insulted
And slighted, they refused to give an inch.
When push came to shove they would feel the pinch.
They might have been wiser, in retrospect,
To agree terms. The least they could expect
Was to have earned some measure of respect
From their own colleagues in the TUC.

So the strike was called off, to the great glee
Of the government. The obstinacy
Of the mineworkers, as many saw it,
Operated to the clear benefit
Of the owners, who were let off the hook.
They now continued, playing by the book,
To resist all modernisation,
Reform or reorganisation.
Baldwin enjoyed a new sensation:
Out of the blue a true British hero.
All he had done was to go with the flow.

The mining industry in crisis

Union morale had reached a new low.
It was not just the miners who were sore.
Other workers who had challenged the law
Found that their own jobs were less than secure,
As a consequence of strike action.
The railwaymen watched in stupefaction
As their employers imposed penalties
And new terms of employment, if you please,
On those men returning to work. A fudge,
Sadly. Still the miners refused to budge.
They carried on their strike. Baldwin, you see,
Felt he could not support one industry,
And not another. Many pits, he knew,
Were unviable, but what could he do?
To wean mining "from the breast of the state" –
That's how Baldwin put it, at any rate –
Was his task. He refused to intervene.
The owners were crowing (rather obscene),
Confident of ultimate victory.

The miners starved. Why, is no mystery.
After six long months their great industry
Was on its knees. And so indeed, alack,
Were the miners themselves. They were forced back,
Their hours and wages under attack.

Increased hours needed legislation.
The government had no hesitation
In authorising an eight-hour day.
When it came to the question of pay,
There were cuts all round. The mines, remember,
Were running at a loss. In December,
The Miners' Federation caved in.
This was a dispute they would never win.

Somewhat to the Prime Minister's chagrin   **1927**
(Or so I assume), the following year
A measure was passed, affording scant cheer
To the TUC. The Trade Disputes Act
Testified to the dispiriting fact
That Baldwin had succumbed to his right wing.

Remember Macquisten? The very thing
That this wretched man had sought to force through
Became the law of the land. Nothing new:
Baldwin was riding the crest of a wave,
So he copped out. What a way to behave.
Trade Unionists had now to opt in,
In writing to boot (all thanks to Baldwin),
Before paying the political levy.
The Tories had won the right to get heavy.

A footnote. The general strike 'crisis'
Proved to be something of a catharsis.
A simple truth that it's easy to miss
Is that the numbers of those on strike fell,
After '26 (a difficult spell),
By two thirds for each of the next ten years.
This, to some extent, was down to the fears
Of the TUC (and men like Bevin),
Namely that to antagonise Baldwin,
And his ilk, was a futile exercise.
Better, by far, to seek to compromise,
To conciliate, and work together.

The much improved political weather
Ensured that the average working man
Was better off (over a three-year span,
Up to '29) than ever before.
Rates of pay remained stable. Furthermore,
The cost of living fell by fifteen points.

A miner's life

The one statistic that still disappoints
Is that the miners, heading for a fall,
Failed to share in this 'affluence' at all.
Writing a decade later, George Orwell
Had a deplorable story to tell
Of a miner's life: the conditions
Down the pit; the worn-out traditions
Of employment; the dire rates of pay;
The agony suffered, day after day,
Shift upon shift, to provide us with coal.

A simple observer was Orwell's role.
Read *The Road to Wigan Pier*, I urge you.
His report, every single word true,
Of the working life of a miner… Well,
It was his "own mental picture of hell".
The heat, the noise, confusion, foul air,
The confined space… But it was getting there,

Depression and the Shadow of War

To the coal face, that took him by surprise.
How, of course, could it have been otherwise,
As Orwell later came to realise?
A miner might have to travel three miles
From pit head to coal face. But what still riles
Is that the journey, cramped and bent double,
Was not part of his shift. For his trouble,
The miner's seven-hour day began –
Or eight, according to the owners' plan –
Only when he started work. A stranger,
Like Orwell, was alert to the danger
Of pit explosions and accidents.

The miners themselves (this has to make sense)
Appeared to become accustomed to it –
The risk, I mean. Disasters, down the pit,
Were commonplace. A sober estimate
Put the chance of escaping injury,
Over forty years in the industry,
At seven to one against. Hold your breath:
The risk, for miners, of escaping death
Was twenty to one. And a miner's pay,
In the thirties? The going rate, per day
(Or per shift), might total, on average,
Nine shillings. Now that's quite a decent wage,
Believe it or not, if he worked all year.
But the summer season brought little cheer.
Demand would slacken, with workers laid off.
The weekly wage was a spit and a cough
(Compared to winter) in warmer weather.

Taking all circumstances together,
The gross earnings in 1934,
For a miner, kept the wolf from the door,
But only barely. Deduct insurance,
And the hire (this beyond endurance)

Of his Davy lamp from the company,
The Benevolent Fund, Union Fee –
All the miner's responsibility –
And his pitiful lot is plain to see.

I have written enough. I can't compete
With George Orwell. His picture is complete.
Do read the book, *The Road to Wigan Pier.*
I can't do proper justice to it here.

Poverty in Britain

In another chapter, beyond compare,
Orwell charts the hopelessness and despair
Among the poorer classes: how they live,
The state of their houses. May God forgive,
I say, the politicians. Baldwin
First visited (now I call this a sin)

A row of working-class slums in Dundee
In 1925 – yes, really!
Full marks, at least, for complacency.
The PM, it appears, got quite a fright.
"I never saw," he confessed, "such a sight."
He'd not imagined it before, of course,
But "the whole thing came to me with such force".
Five or six members of one family
In one room: "think of the children!" Frankly,
Having been Prime Minister for two years,
These were little more than crocodile tears.
Neville Chamberlain laboured hard, it's true,
For change. But what did Stanley Baldwin do?
Nothing much. Sadly, this was nothing new.

Chamberlain's reforms

I never warmed to Baldwin's attitude.
The self-proclaimed "master of platitude",
He reached his peak of popularity
In '26. Mobbed, quite literally,
Outside 10 Downing Street, honest Stanley
Could do no wrong. The government's record,
However, was weak. The Reform Award,
Had there been one, would have been Chamberlain's.

He was worth at least a dozen Baldwins.
His '29 Local Government Act
Was born of a spirit that Stanley lacked –
A revolution, and that's a fact.
In England and Wales the reformed counties,
And boroughs, became the authorities
For almost all local activities:
Town and country planning, housing, welfare,
Slum clearance – a new broom everywhere…
Education, public health, transport,
The police, even (as an afterthought)

Child care and maternity services.
This, of course, is only a synopsis.
Most of these reforms survive to this day.
Hats off to Neville Chamberlain, I say.

No more war?

In foreign affairs there was some progress,
Though the Kellogg-Briand Pact, I confess,
Was all words. Signed in 1928,   **1928**
It appeared to offer peace on a plate.
The United States had agreed with France
Never to go to war. Well, at first glance,
Who could balk at that? They opened the door
To other nations renouncing war,
With the result that thirteen more countries,
Including Britain, signed up. Hostilities
Were 'outlawed', although not (and this made sense)
Measures taken purely in self-defence.
This, of course, was simple pie in the sky –
No means of enforcement the reason why.

The Dominions

One policy that made much better sense
Came of the Imperial Conference,
In 1926. Independence:
This had been enjoyed for years, in practice,
By the Dominions, but it was this,
Independent status, that they now sought –
In clear, defined terms. The campaign was fought,
With great energy, by Mackenzie King,
The Canadian PM. Anything,
He declared, was better than subservience
To Britain's Parliament. This, in essence,
The conference (chaired by the Earl of Balfour,
The Lord President) could not have favoured more.

Defined as "autonomous communities",
The Dominions (including, if you please,
The Irish Free State) would remain united –
All the parties expressed themselves delighted –
"By a common allegiance to the Crown".
Balfour, an ex-Prime Minister of renown,
Scored a win for Britain and for himself.
As "members of the British Commonwealth",
The free Dominions earned the respect,
And the status, they'd been led to expect.
The Statute of Westminster ('31)
Gave the measure legal effect. Deal done.

Women's suffrage

To the great relief of everyone,
Women now won the vote at twenty-one.

Universal adult suffrage at last,
Though the Labour Party remained aghast
That the old university franchise
(The business one, too) remained – far from wise.
But the Equal Franchise Act, piloted
By Joynson-Hicks, the right-wing, bigoted
Home Secretary, was a welcome move,
And few there were who were slow to approve.

Some twenty years later (in '48),
A sure case of too little, too late,
Plural voting was at last abolished.
I know you'll be suitably astonished,
As was I, to learn that up until then,
Half a million voters, mainly men,
Could cast two votes at an election.
So, a move in the right direction.

'Safety first'

The government was running out of steam.
Another term for Baldwin? He could dream,
For Stanley was supremely confident.

The outcome (almost without precedent)
Eluded him. He was fit for the fray,
Or so he believed. Election day
Was in late spring, the 30th of May,   **1929**
And the omens looked good, I have to say.

Baldwin dared his rivals to do their worst.
His comfortable slogan, 'Safety First',
Would appeal to voters, or so he thought.
Trust your PM, an honourable sort!
Why risk a change? Short on policy, true,
He hoped they'd stick with the devil they knew.

The Liberals were champing at the bit.
Unemployment? Lloyd George would conquer it.
For Ll.G. had taken the reins again,
After Asquith's retirement. Forget pain:
The Liberal Party would take the strain.
He promised to reduce unemployment
Within a year, with the redeployment
Of funds to schemes of public investment:
Housing schemes, electrification,
Telephones, and the renovation
Of the countryside. Backed up, for his pains,
By the economist, John Maynard Keynes –
The two had never exactly been friends,
But both were now eager to make amends –
Lloyd George was bursting with ideas, schemes
And plans, the stuff of political dreams.

Stanley Baldwin warned the electorate
Not to get carried away. Yes, you bet!
The leader with the best policies yet
Was met with ignorant criticism,
Scare-mongering and blind cynicism.
Labour, under MacDonald, were content
Simply to appear fit for government.
Their manifesto, as far as it went,
Was bland – not much better than the Tories'.

Baldwin defeated

In one of politics' hard-luck stories,
The Liberals were squeezed – yes, yet again.
They fought an imaginative campaign
And won nineteen extra seats – not a gain,
I regret, of any practical use.
Now, I refuse to make any excuse
For 'first past the post'. It's simply absurd,
But it did for Lloyd George, you have my word.

The Liberals won twenty-eight *per cent*
Of the vote (not a great score, though decent),
But a paltry ten *per cent* of the seats –
This, in effect, the mother of defeats,
From which they never recovered. Labour –
A tally MacDonald was to savour –
Managed fewer votes than Baldwin's Tories,
But deprived them of their former glories,
Winning twenty-seven more seats! In fact,
Three hundred thousand votes, to be exact,
Divided them: that's a lead, by a nose,
Of one and a half *per cent.* I suppose,
To be fair, Baldwin had every right
To feel cheated. He had fought a good fight,
And lost – at least according to the rules.

The PM, never one to suffer fools,
Did the proper thing and gave up office.
However, it was a poisoned chalice
He passed to MacDonald. The stage was set
For high drama. You have seen nothing yet.

Noël Coward

The twenties were the defining decade
For Noël Coward. The old guard were dismayed
(Or purported to be) by his louche style,
His clipped vowels and his enigmatic smile,
But he won the race, by a country mile,
To become the new talent: dramatist,
Producer, composer and lyricist,
Actor and director – that's quite a list.
He made his stage *début* in *The Great Name*,
Playing a pageboy. Noël's road to fame
Began early (he was twelve at the time).
Stage-struck after seeing a pantomime,

Aladdin, in Kingston (1903),
The boy was set, you can take it from me,
On a stage career. It simply made sense.
No figure had a greater influence,
In theatre, between the wars, than he.

His first sure-fire success was, strangely,
A serious piece, his play *The Vortex*.
It dealt with drug abuse (a code for sex?),
The first drama in England so to do.
Coward was challenging; Coward was new.

The Vortex (Noël himself in the lead)
Opened in triumph and, set to succeed,
Transferred from Hampstead to London's West End,
Where the young playwright's 'talent to offend'
Drew in the crowds. The play was a huge hit.
Noël Coward had arrived, and that was it!

Rhyming History

The Vortex? Well, I can't say I'm smitten,
But the funniest play ever written –
Or up in the top ten comedies, at least –
Must be *Hay Fever*, a veritable feast.
Witty, refreshing, winsome and relaxed,
The audience is never overtaxed,
And this was Coward's secret: so easy,
Superficially bright and breezy,
Yet true to a T – and never cheesy.

He took Broadway by storm. New Yorkers knew
A star when they saw one: *Easy Virtue,*
Hay Fever, The Vortex, three plays, no less –
"A violent and glittering success,"
In Coward's own words! His revues, to boot,
Were a knockout: *London Calling!* (a hoot),
This Year of Grace, all-singing, all-dancing,
With music to die for – life-enhancing,
Magical, extravagant, entrancing.
Although the revues are rarely revived,
Some of the songs from these shows have survived,
The melodious *A Room with a View*
And *Poor Little Rich Girl*, to name but two.

The romantic musical, *Bitter Sweet*,
Made Noël's run of successes complete.
It excited James Agate (quite a feat:
The most severe of critics), who called it
"A thundering good job". That meant a hit!
One of the numbers, *I'll See You Again*,
Is sung to this day, a haunting refrain.

His triumphs in the twenties, in the main,
Set the trend. One masterpiece that survives,
Regularly revived, is *Private Lives* –
Quintessential Coward: Elyot Chase,
And his ex-wife Amanda, face to face,

Depression and the Shadow of War

On their respective honeymoons... Sybil
(Elyot's new wife, inclined to quibble –
Coward's wordplay, not mine) and Victor Prynne,
Amanda's husband. It never wears thin,
This subtle comedy: China ("very big"),
Norfolk ("very flat"). Shallow? Who cares a fig?
Besides, it is far from superficial.
For all that the plot is artificial,
When Amanda's hearty husband, Victor,
Says, "I'm glad I'm normal", she's not so sure.
Victor and Sybil are shown the door.

Amanda and Elyot declare war,
Both driven to the end of their tether,
But fated to spend their lives together –
The worst of matrimonial weather...
Or the best? Coward leaves us to decide:
A simple life, or a rollicking ride?

Arnold Bennett called him (I have to say,
Some compliment) the "Congreve of his day".

Robert Stephens and Maggie Smith, a dream,
Starred in *Private Lives,* the ideal team.
I also saw the great Alan Rickman,
Opposite the superb Lindsay Duncan.
They won a Tony Award, on Broadway,
For Best Revival. Well deserved, I say.

Private Lives, written in 1930,
Was a hit. Starting to get shirty,
However, was the Lord Chamberlain.
Design for Living? Coward couldn't win.
The wretched man got his blue pencil out
And hacked it to ribbons. Without a doubt,
The play featured an amoral trio
(Bisexual?), presented with brio,

Rhyming History

Energy, wit, vivacity and flair.
A licence to perform? He wouldn't dare.

Coward cocked him a snook. Did Noël care?
Did he buffalo! He was not all talk:
The play opened to plaudits in New York.
It didn't reach London 'til '39,
When it proved a hit: "perfect... divine..."
The Lord Chamberlain finally backed down.
Noël, again, was the talk of the town.

The war years brought fame of another sort.
Noël Coward succumbed, as he felt he ought,
To patriotic sentiment. The need
Was for uplifting films. *This Happy Breed*
And *In Which We Serve* were both massive hits,
While *Blithe Spirit* had the public in fits –
First a play, then a film. Trevor Howard
And Celia Johnson (vintage Coward)
Starred in *Brief Encounter,* still, to this day,
A drama to cherish, a moving play.

Post-war, the age of the 'angry young man'
Gave him troubled years. The decline began
With pieces such as *Relative Values*
And *Quadrille,* both seen as rather stale news,
Old-fashioned and sadly out of date.
His career picked up, at any rate,
In 1964. Olivier
Asked him to direct his funniest play,
Hay Fever, at the National. This,
Starring Edith Evans as Judith Bliss,
Put him back on the map. Aged seventy,
'The Master' was knighted. "Heavenly,"
Was his response (so I'd imagine).
Noël Coward played hard, and he played to win.

Depression and the Shadow of War

A. A. Milne

In the twenties another dramatist,
Hugely popular and not to be missed,
Was A. A. Milne. He is famous today,
Of course, not for *The Dover Road,* a play
Rarely revived, *Mr. Pim Passes By,*
Or *Toad of Toad Hall.* These exemplify
His success as a playwright, all too true,
But it's his famous bear, Winnie-the-Pooh,
Who won the hearts of generations.

One of those overnight sensations,
Winnie-the-Pooh, featuring Kanga, Roo,
And the Bear of Little Brain himself, Pooh,
Piglet and Eeyore, was an instant hit.
His son didn't like it one little bit,
Christopher Robin – well, the fame that is,
Although in time he learned to live with this.
Most of the animals, including Pooh,
Who had come from Harrods (I promise you),
Lived in Christopher Robin's toy cupboard.
Only Rabbit and Owl, I've discovered,
Were native to the Hundred Acre Wood.

Winnie-the-Pooh (as a children's book should)
Has a lasting appeal for adults too.
The wise old 'Wol', the dependable Pooh,
Busy Rabbit, ever-gloomy Eeyore,
Bossy Kanga and (easy to ignore)
Little Piglet are figures to adore.

Then *The House at Pooh Corner* offers more,
With the sudden arrival of Tigger –
Bolder, bouncier, brasher and bigger.
The tales are timeless: for Eeyore's birthday –
A pot of honey (rather, I should say,

An empty honey pot) and a balloon
(Or its remnants), although both, very soon,
Become the perfect present; or, at last,
Finding out what Tiggers like for breakfast;
Or Pooh coming down to earth with a bump,
When he and Piglet meet a Heffalump;
Or hunting the Woozle (you have to laugh);
Or Kanga giving wee Piglet a bath...
Simple stories. You'll gather I'm a fan.
A. A. Milne – a most remarkable man.

The best of book illustrators

Illustrators are worth their weight in gold.
E. H. Shepard, if I may be so bold,
Was the finest exemplar of his craft.
When I first heard the stories, how I laughed.

Shepard's superb drawings I remember still:
Piglet and his grandfather, TRESPASSERS WILL;

Poor Pooh with the honey pot stuck on his head;
When Kanga lost Roo, bathing Piglet instead;
Tracking the Woozle, its prints in the snow;
Eeyore in the thistles; Wol in full flow...
The drawings are playful, witty and strong –
A talent like this, he couldn't go wrong.
E. H. Shepard, Quentin Blake, John Partridge –
To praise their efforts is my privilege,
Illustrators of genius, all three,
But J. P. of course particularly.

MacDonald's minority government

Back to politics. In a minority,
MacDonald could boast some 'seniority',
Nonetheless. His position was stronger,
Second time round, and he lasted for longer.
With more Labour MPs than ever before –
Two hundred and eighty-seven was their score –
And with twenty-seven more than the Tories,
This was hardly the worst of horror stories.
Baldwin was 'relaxed' in opposition
And, as for the Liberals' position,
The last thing they wanted now was a new poll.
Ramsay MacDonald, for once, was on a roll.

MacDonald's ministers

However, in circumstances such as these,
A programme of sustained left-wing policies
Was never on the cards. This suited him fine.
A moderate, he knew where to draw the line.
As leader of Labour, MacDonald's command
Was strong. Any disagreeable demand,
From the left, he could readily brush aside.
Never one for political suicide

Rhyming History

(Though watch this space), MacDonald's new Cabinet
Was right of centre – cautious, moderate,
And with some experience. Philip Snowden.
That most orthodox (and determined) of men,
Returned, as Chancellor, to the Treasury.
Arthur Henderson (Foreign Secretary)
Gave MacDonald some headaches. Nevertheless,
He proved an outstanding (and surprise) success.
J. H. Thomas, a key MacDonald ally,
Was appointed Lord Privy Seal. Do or die,
His brief was to tackle that terrible scourge,
Unemployment. The sad victim of a purge,
John Wheatley, a clear and undisputed star
First time round, the finest minister by far,
Was regrettably omitted from the list.
Too popular, perhaps? Well, you get the gist.

The new Minister of Health, Arthur Greenwood,
Stepped into his shoes and proved a force for good,
One of the enduring successes, in fact,
Of the new government. Greenwood's Housing Act,
Building on Wheatley's earlier achievements –
An imaginative set of agreements
Between the builders, local authorities
And government, with the help of subsidies –
Led to a massive programme of slum clearance.
Thanks, in the main, to Greenwood's perseverance,
More slums were torn down and replaced, in five years,
Than in the past half-century, it appears.
The trend continued after he left office,
But Greenwood laid the solid groundwork for this.

One particular appointment to savour
Was MacDonald's new Minister of Labour,
Margaret Bondfield, the first woman ever
To sit in a Cabinet. Able, clever

And resolute, she began her career
As a salesgirl in Brighton. Give her a cheer.
Margaret was never popular, sadly,
But on the whole she didn't do too badly.
The first female Privy Counsellor, to boot,
She never had to hire a morning suit.

Foreign affairs and disarmament

In the field of foreign affairs, Henderson
Earned high regard, but MacDonald was the one,
The crafty old devil, who hogged the limelight.
Elbowing Henderson aside (far from bright),
MacDonald travelled extensively abroad,
The very first Prime Minister on record
To visit the United States. A huge hit,
It was agreed that MacDonald did his bit
In thawing Anglo-US relations –
Intimate, fireside conversations
With the President: a first, I have to say,
Though run-of-the-mill and commonplace today.

They fêted him with a ticker-tape parade
Through New York. Of such events, legends are made.
"We all owe him a great debt of gratitude,"
Baldwin enthused (the master of platitude).

Disarmament talks, both parties decided,
Should take place in London. And who presided?
MacDonald. The PM also took the lead –
With all his experience, he felt the need –
At a Round Table conference in London
On Indian affairs. What of Henderson?
He seems, to his credit, to have kept his cool –
Not his observance, as a general rule.
Labour's Foreign Secretary was no fool:
He established a strong reputation,
On his own terms, for negotiation,
And tact, in international affairs.
The French may well have been taken unawares
When, although made to jump through several hoops,
He secured the withdrawal of Allied troops
From the Rhineland, five years ahead of schedule.

For Henderson was not one of the old school.
He led from the front. He resolved, without fuss,
To restore relations (a distinct plus)
With Soviet Russia. Outstanding debts?
Pah! Despondent talk of military threats?
Forget it. Arthur Henderson brought to bear
A creative spirit. A breath of fresh air.

Wages and pensions

To return to the home front, a Coal Mines Act –
A field requiring some degree of tact –
Prescribed minimum wages and, at long last,
Improved pit safety. The owners were aghast:

Depression and the Shadow of War

Imagine the upheaval... and the expense...
Labour persisted. It made absolute sense.

A new Pensions Act (1929)
Granted pensions (an encouraging sign)
To the mass of widows, children and old folk –
Some half a million, no word of a joke –
Who had failed to qualify previously.
This long-overdue measure passed easily,
With Liberal support. More progressive schemes
For the unemployed (widely welcomed, it seems)
In Labour's Unemployment Insurance Act
Were introduced. The worker (laid off, or sacked)
Was now better protected, and that's a fact.

Depression and unemployment

When MacDonald's new government took office,
The omens looked good. Though nobody knew this,
The slight drop in unemployment, year on year,
Was less encouraging than it would appear.
Exports were on the rise, though again, I fear,
The upturn proved a bitter illusion.
Within five short months, all was confusion.

The Wall Street crash, in October/November –
The worst crisis anyone could remember –
Had a hugely destructive knock-on effect.
America's lending, as you might expect,
Dried up. The fragile German economy
Tottered, compromising the prosperity
(Such as it was) and the productivity
Of central Europe. A trade depression
Took hold, and this led to the impression –
It's often a case of confidence, you see –
That the government was facing bankruptcy.

Rhyming History

Unemployment figures for 1930
Paint a dismal picture: in January,
One and a half million; by the summer
Nearly two million, an awesome number;
While the figure rose, in 1931,
To over two and three-quarter million.

For people in work, wages remained stable.
They clung on to their jobs, if they were able,
But for the unemployed the outlook was grim.
As for MacDonald, they'd put their trust in him,
And as far as they could fathom he had failed,
Their perilous hopes for the future derailed.
As British Prime Minister, what could he do?
It soon became clear that he hadn't a clue.

A junior minister, Oswald Mosley,
A new Labour recruit, in January
Drew up a detailed plan for recovery:
A huge investment programme, over three years,
Of public works (not as mad as it appears),
Along the lines earlier proposed by Keynes.
Poor Mosley found himself sidelined for his pains.
Raising millions in loans to pay for schemes
Such as roads and new industries? In your dreams!
Mosley's ideas were barely debated.
They came to nothing. Overlooked, frustrated
And angry, he resigned. Snowden was to blame.
Reckless government spending? Not in his name.

The Chancellor's mantra? A balanced budget.
This he believed, and he refused to fudge it.
MacDonald, Heaven help him, was all at sea,
So attentive to foreign affairs was he.
Lloyd George commented, with cruel irony,
That the PM, quite simply, was "too busy

"To do his job". What of the economy?
His answer was to set up a committee,
Under Sir George May, to report on the state
Of public finances. Too little, too late.

Financial crisis

For by the time Sir George published his Report,   **1931**
In July, many a battle had been fought,
And lost. Unemployment was still on the rise.
Even the government's Liberal allies –
The Tories too, to nobody's great surprise –
Demanded immediate economies.
May's published findings predicted, if you please,
An overall current account deficit –
The City of London nearly had a fit –
Of one hundred and twenty million pounds.
This afforded the Chancellor ample grounds
For prescribing strong medicine: swingeing cuts
In public expenditure, no ifs, no buts.

Taxation increases, on a large scale,
Were counterproductive and sure to fail –
So Snowden believed. Part of the deficit
Could be met in this way. The rich would be hit,
But so would 'confidence'. Where did Snowden sit?
Certainly not on the fence! The unemployed
Must pay their share. Confidence would be destroyed
If the cost of unemployment benefit
Was not reduced. Let the workers do their bit.

Then came a sudden run on Britain's credit.
First the Austrian bank, *Kreditanstalt*, failed.
Germany's economy was then derailed,
As German banks sought to ride to its rescue.
Investors in Europe (what else could they do?)

Withdrew their funds. The trickle became a flood.
Attempting to nip the crisis in the bud,
The City advanced large sums to Germany,
In a bid to shore up her economy.
The strategy failed. The money was all lost.
The Bank of England was left to count the cost.

The French, whose reserves were surprisingly strong,
Loathed the Germans. British policy was wrong!
So the French withdrew their credit from London,
With no proper regard for the damage done.
In August there was a huge run on the pound.
In a single week Britain lost (in the round)
Eleven million of the Bank's money
And ten million (this was far from funny)
Of reserves, borrowed to defend, we are told,
'Parity' – *viz.* keeping the pound pegged to gold.

For the Gold Standard, it was broadly agreed,
Was Britain's lifeline in her hour of need.
Suspend gold, and the country would face collapse:
Hyperinflation, bankruptcy perhaps,
And economic ruin. Without a doubt,
The financial options were running out.
Some sixty million in foreign exchange,
And gold, had been lost in a month. Now it's strange,
But nobody listened to John Maynard Keynes.
Despite all the arguments, stresses and strains,
Keynes was not an economist to kow-tow
To the Gold Standard. Yet for all his know-how,
He was ignored. Only a balanced budget
Would do the trick, and Snowden bit the bullet.

The crisis was the threat to Britain's credit –
Pressing, overwhelming and immediate.
Snowden, to reduce the budget deficit,
Saw a cut in unemployment benefit,
Of ten *per cent*, as the only way out.
Those paid by the state (to clear up any doubt)
Would also bear the brunt: the armed services,
Judges, government ministers… It was this
(A ten *per cent* cut all round) that made it fair.
Teachers fared worse (however did Snowden dare?),
Losing fifteen *per cent* of their salaries –
Clearly one of society's luxuries!

Collapse of the Labour government

To nobody's surprise, the Cabinet split.
Nine (out of nineteen) were having none of it.
Arthur Henderson, for one, threatened to quit.
Deadlock. The TUC also had a fit.
Any cut in unemployment insurance
They strongly opposed – beyond all endurance.

Proposed cuts in social services, too,
Were anathema. What could MacDonald do?
Well, Tories and Liberals, over to you.

The Labour government could not continue.
This MacDonald and all his Cabinet knew.
The Prime Minister had met Stanley Baldwin
And Herbert Samuel (Lloyd George's stand-in,
Who was ill) to update them on the crisis.
The most likely outcome, in his view, was this:
A Tory-Liberal coalition.

The Libs had a better proposition.
With no hope of reviving former glories,
They dreaded eclipse by the pesky Tories,
Anticipating a pretty rocky ride
In such an alliance – certain suicide,
Moreover, at the polls. It was Samuel,
Therefore, a good, old-fashioned Liberal,
Who proposed a National Government.
Baldwin supported the notion, content,
For once in his life, to play second fiddle.
You may ask why. No particular riddle:
Why should the Tories be caught in the middle,
And be forced to bear responsibility
For possible national bankruptcy?

The best outcome, as far as Baldwin could see,
Was to join forces. MacDonald was the man!
Let the PM bat on, and carry the can.

A National Government

Now King George the Fifth was a MacDonald fan.
Baldwin, Samuel and the King were happy:
Form a new government, and make it snappy.

Depression and the Shadow of War

MacDonald consented, as he knew he must –
This was a question of honour, and trust.
As early as the 24th of August,
The new National Government was formed.
Cabinet members were politely informed
That the King had graciously accepted
Their resignations – not unexpected.

Three of MacDonald's former colleagues, just three,
Joined him in the new Cabinet: Lord Sankey
Remained as Lord Chancellor; MacDonald's friend,
J. H. Thomas, loyal and true to the end,
Was Dominions Secretary. The post,
It goes without saying, that mattered the most
Was the Treasury. Philip Snowden stayed on,
Though Chamberlain would soon take up the baton.

Neville, for now, had done quite well for himself,
Back in his own job as Minister of Health.
The deputy Prime Minister, in effect,
Was Stanley Baldwin, no less than you'd expect.
Samuel was the new Home Secretary.
It appeared all parties were happy, very.

The Cabinet was small, numbering just ten:
Four Labour, four Tory, two Liberal men.
And there let us leave them to sort themselves out –
They'd a mountain to climb, no shadow of doubt.

One postscript. Ramsay MacDonald was expelled
From the Labour Party. The post he had held,
That of leader, went to Arthur Henderson,
The job he'd long coveted, all said and done.
As for Ramsay, Labour never forgave him.
He had burnt his boats. Could history save him?
We shall see, but I won't get carried away.
In any case, it's hardly for me to say.

Rhyming History

Britain in the 1920s

It's time to give the decade some perspective,
With a broad 1920s retrospective.

The country was struggling. Nothing new.
The Labour government hadn't a clue,
Nor had the Tories. So what did they do?
They sat on their hands. This was sadly true.

Transport

Yet in some parts the economy grew,
Down south, for example. There's a surprise!
For starters, road traffic was on the rise.
Like the railways of yore, the motor car
Transformed Britain. Travel, however far,
Was no longer dependent on the train.
Transport in cities and towns, in the main,
Take it or leave it, had long been the tram.

That new phenomenon, the traffic jam,
Was born of the tram's replacement, the bus,
And the huge increase in cars. Now, to us,
The downside of the tram is obvious:
Fixed tracks and lack of flexibility,
Whereas the great joy of the bus, clearly,
And the car, is that there is no limit
To their range of travel. Good, isn't it!

The two hundred thousand cars registered
In 1920 rose, from what I've heard,
To one million by 1930,
An incredible increase, certainly.
Hefty sums were spent on road maintenance:
Given the numbers, this made perfect sense.

The motor car too had a marked effect –
Rather more, I think, than you might expect –
On the growth of our towns and cities.

It bred urban sprawl (a thousand pities),
As car owners could live with their spouses
(And their two-point-four children) in houses
Nearer roads, away from a railway line.
The railways went into rapid decline.
The new commuter? It suited him fine.
Modern estates sprang up along the road:
"Toot-toot!" (that's a homage to Mr. Toad).

Anyone over seventeen could drive.
There weren't any driving tests (saints alive!)
Until 1934. My own dad,
Whose driving, I reckon, was not so bad,

Rhyming History

Was still at the wheel at eighty-one –
A few near misses, but no harm done –
Having never been asked to take a test.
Roundabouts bothered him, tricky at best.

Roads had an impact on new industries.
In earlier days, Britain's factories
Had been built where there was easy transport:
Railways lines, canals and routes of that sort –
Or perhaps near a pit, or a sea port.
This was now no longer necessary:
Roads shaped the new pattern of industry.
A factory could be built anywhere.
Men in Blackburn, or Colne, could only stare,
Their industries defunct. Pain and despair:
Heavy unemployment everywhere.
It's odd, but people are rarely aware
Of the grim effect of the motor car.
It brought grief to thousands, but there you are.

On the other hand (no need to ask why),
The motor industry was on a high.
The resurgent, lighter industries, too,
Enjoyed the advantage. Bring on the new!
Modern furniture, electrical goods,
China ware… Was Britain out of the woods?
No, but although these changes spelt the doom
Of the older world, it was not all gloom.

For service industries were doing well.
Wage levels, in general, hardly fell
In this sector. If you ran a hotel,
It seems, you were laughing. Even today,
Some folk don't expect holidays with pay,
But this was beginning to be the trend –
For the seaside landlady, a godsend!

Entertainment: radio, cinema and theatre

This was also the age of radio.
By 1939, I'll have you know,
Nine homes in ten owned a wireless set,
And all paid the licence fee (yes, you bet…).

The most popular entertainment yet,
However, was the cinema. Forget,
Sadly, the theatre, the music hall
And variety. Films eclipsed them all.

Picture houses popped up everywhere,
A popular antidote to despair,
And the dark shadow of unemployment.
There was no better form of enjoyment
Than the cinema. Some forty *per cent*
Of Liverpool's population went
(Yes, forty) once a week – and twenty-five
Went twice, no doubt to keep their spirits alive.

Rhyming History

Theatre died a death. Old companies,
Touring the provinces, were on their knees.
Only a few major towns and cities
Could sustain the drama. Whole families
Deserted the playhouse, in the twenties,
For the picture palaces. Some survived,
But as soon as the 'talkies' had arrived,
Their death knell was sounded. The golden age
Of the 'Empires' was past. All the rage
Were the modern epics from Hollywood.
Live entertainment had vanished for good.

Priestley's English pilgrimage

For a taste of what touring used to be,
And the strange world that was variety,
Look up the novel by J. B. Priestley,
An entertaining read, *Lost Empires.*
It's the commitment one most admires,
The weekly slog. Hardly life-enhancing,
But the picture he paints is entrancing.

In his definitive *English Journey,*
Priestley records the state of the country
In the autumn of 1933.
What, he asks, did it mean to be English,
In those testing times? From start to finish,
You'll be gripped. Observant, steady and wise,
On every page you'll find a surprise.

He began his study in Southampton,
Taking a motor coach out of London,
A first for Priestley. Impressed by its speed,
And level of comfort, he was intrigued.
The coach appeared to offer luxury
To both rich and poor. One discovery

Depression and the Shadow of War

Was the long line of factories he saw
On the road (presumably the A4)
Out of the city: buildings of concrete,
Glass and chromium plate, compact and neat –
These in stark contrast to the factories
Of his Bradford youth, with their tall chimneys
And blackened walls, built in oppressive squares,
Forbidding and bleak. Taken unawares,
He understood they catered for all tastes:
"Bathing costumes, potato crisps, tooth pastes,
"Fire extinguishers…" Forget the wastes,
For a moment, of Yorkshire and the north,
These were new to him. So Priestley set forth
For Southampton. The great depression –
This, at least, was his first impression –
Appeared to have passed it by, a fine port,
Thriving, wealthy and still of some import.
He saw shops, of course, of the lower sort,
And some dismal housing but, on the whole,
People looked prosperous and on a roll.

On to Bristol, *via* Salisbury.
The first sight of that cathedral city
He aptly describes as "a noble view
"Of England". Pay a visit, I urge you:
Its slim spire, "like a pointed finger,
"Faintly luminous". He didn't linger,
He needed to press on… But not before
He took note of a small crowd that he saw,
Of unemployed, waiting (was that so strange?)
Outside the Salisbury Labour Exchange –
"As pitiful… as ever I have seen".
Perhaps there was something faintly obscene,
For such an ancient, affluent city,
In a sight such as this. More's the pity,
This was merely an early warning sign –
Enough to send the shivers down your spine –

Rhyming History

Of what lay in store. For this, I regret,
Was only the start. You've seen nothing yet.

Bristol was a hive of activity,
"Old and alive", prosperous and busy.
Priestley was struck by the Wills family,
Whose world-famous tobacco factory
Brought them security, wealth and renown.
Yet they lived locally, on Clifton Down,
Rather than turn away from the city,
As did other captains of industry
In places rather less salubrious.

Swindon was next. Priestley was dubious.
The Great Western Railway had been based there.
Now the town wore a melancholy air,
Not exactly on the edge of despair,
But monotonous houses, in squat rows,
Dingy and dull, built, as the need arose,
For Victorian artisans. Swindon,
On a damp, dark night in early autumn,
Was a doleful prospect, all said and done.

The Cotswolds! Upper and Lower Slaughter,
Burford, Broadway, Bourton-on-the-Water,
Clearly "the most English and the least spoiled
"Of our countrysides". The craftsmen still toiled,
Like old George, expert in dry-stone-walling,
In his seventies – wages appalling,
But a labour of love, close to his heart.
The Cotswold stone buildings are works of art;
As for the scenery, where do you start?
Just as well, Priestley writes with a wry smile,
Gentle irony his disarming style,
That no coal deposits were discovered
In these hills. They'd never have recovered.

Depression and the Shadow of War

To Coventry next, one of those cities
That had kept pace, over the centuries,
With modern trends: in the middle ages
Cotton, then gloves and buttons (in stages);
Then ribbons in the eighteenth century;
Then bikes and sewing machines aplenty,
In the nineteenth. Now, in the present day,
By the twenties and thirties anyway,
It was radio sets and machine tools.
The people of Coventry were no fools.

With new technology they raised the bar,
For this was the age of the motor car.
Yet for all the wealth the city enjoyed,
There were still 12,000 men unemployed.

Then the 'Black Country', *via* Birmingham.
That great city was something of a sham,
For behind the municipal splendour,
There was little else on the agenda
But "mile after mile of mean dinginess" –
Areas of depressing ugliness:
Not slum housing exactly, but nothing
To give the place more than an empty ring.

Located to the north of the city,
And out to the west, lay the Black Country.
Approaching through Smethwick and Oldbury,
Priestley made his weary way to Dudley,
Which he describes as "a fantastic place" –
In the sense, I regret, of a disgrace,
Rather than a miracle! Looking down,
From a steep hill overlooking the town,
"Like a smouldering carpet" the country
Lay before him – chimney after chimney,
"An immense hollow of smoke", factory

After factory. What he also found,
To his dismay, were patches of waste ground,
As "shocking" as "open wounds" and "raw sores".
The prospect gave Priestley reason to pause,
To reflect. The earth had been "left gaping
"And bleeding". There could be no escaping
The bitter truth. Ravaged by industry,
The town had been wrecked. What a history.

There was worse to come, far worse to be seen.
'Rusty Lane', West Bromwich. Picture the scene:
The "grimy desolation" of the street.
The squalor, to make the image complete,
Was hideous, hovel after hovel.
Had Dickens portrayed them in a novel,
"Brick by brick", he'd have been laughed out of court.
But this was sad reality, not sport.
People lived there; their children were born there –
The very epitome of despair.
The "whole pomp of government" was a joke.
What did they know of England, the rich folk?
Hold the next economic conference
In Rusty Lane! Now that would make good sense.

Depression and the Shadow of War

Let the complacent delegates be fed
With slabs of brawn, margarine and dry bread.
The heart of England, Mother of the Free,
Legendary Land of Hope and Glory,
Would be revealed in all her majesty:
Viz. poverty, hunger and penury.
Hats off, I say, to John Boynton Priestley.

We'll skip through Leicester and Nottingham, where,
For his sins, he visited the Goose Fair –
Tawdry tat, glare and din everywhere.
Not a goose to be seen! Those attending
Were the only geese, no use pretending.

Bradford was J. B. Priestley's place of birth.
It's probable that no place on God's earth –
Former centre of wealth and influence –
Better represented the true essence
Of the Industrial Revolution.
Forget for a moment the pollution,
The ruination of the countryside,
The poison and destruction far and wide,
Let's knuckle down and consider the facts.
Northerners, we're told, are fond of brass tacks.
So be it, then. Between 1801 –
Take that date as a sort of starting gun –
And 1901, just a hundred years,
The population grew, it appears,
From 13,000 (a comfortable size)
To 280,000, a rise
Well in excess of 2,000 *per cent.*

Bradford's position was Heaven-sent,
Perfectly placed for the manufacture
Of worsted and woollen goods, which prefer
Soft water (free of lime) for the process
Of washing and dyeing. Anything less

Rhyming History

Would be ruinous. An ample supply
Of such water was at hand. Then, nearby,
Were extensive coalfields. For the great mills,
Energy was essential. No frills,
No nonsense, all this was as mother's milk
To the entrepreneur. Alpaca, silk
And mohair, too, were specialities.
With ideal conditions such as these
For spinning, weaving, finishing, dyeing,
The town prospered without even trying.

Bradford, at the centre of the wool trade,
Was without rival. Its fortune was made.
Dozens of wool merchants were swept away
In the great depression. In its day,
This most profitable of industries,
With over two hundred smoking chimneys,
Was alive from dawn to dusk. Well, not now:
The trade slump was taking its toll, and how.
Export markets had been in slow decline
Since before the War. One worrying sign
Was that those countries with money to spend
Were setting a new and troubling trend:
Flimsier fabrics than Bradford produced
Meant lower prices, with orders reduced.

"One firm after another," Priestley writes,
"Staggered, then crashed." When recession bites,
There is nowhere to hide. Industries die,
With morale low, and unemployment high.*

Bradford was "entirely without charm".
At least Priestley was blunt. Where was the harm?
He took a walk on "a wettish, raw night"
Round the city centre, noting its plight:
Just pub after pub, a depressing sight.

Depression and the Shadow of War

Nothing to do, nobody anywhere,
"A miserable, barbaric affair".
There was nowhere for live music at all.
The old concert venue, St. George's Hall,
Was now a "permanent picture theatre" –
Or another cinema, if you prefer,
As was the fine Theatre Royal, alas.
Forgive me, please, if you consider this crass,
But to close it down? Little less than a crime.
It's where Irving played for the very last time.

I'm aware that I should pick up the pace.
To the Potteries! An ugly place,
Distinctly "shabby", declining apace –
"Neither old and charming, nor bright and new".
Were there compensations? Very few,
Although there was a tip-top bus service.
The people of Stoke-on-Trent deserved this,
For Stoke consisted, believe it or not,
Of six separate towns (rather a lot) –
Not five, as Arnold Bennett informed us.
Whether five, six or seven, why the fuss?
Feeling cut off? Why, just hop on a bus.

---

*Priestley fails to give us the statistics
For Bradford, but they were a lethal mix.
The unemployed for 1929:
Thirteen and a half thousand. Well, that's fine,
Employers would argue (more's the pity).
It's a modest figure, apparently,
For a town of that size. By '33,
The figure had risen, regrettably,
To twenty-two thousand. A tragedy.
This information comes from *Hansard*.
You can look it up. It is not that hard.

Rhyming History

Liverpool was "docks and slums, docks and slums".
Priestley was never one to do the sums,
But he saw "miles of it". As for the Mersey,
Anything "more spectral and melancholy",
As darkness descended, he was yet to see.

Travelling through Bolton, the ugliness,
To him, was calculated to impress,
So complete it was (no understating)
As to be "almost exhilarating".
"Where there's muck, there's money," the saying goes.
Priestley (wryly, one can only suppose),
Never a fellow to be taken in,
Gives the old adage a different spin:
There was still the muck, but not much money –
Sadly true. He was not being funny.

Cotton, the Victorians' pride and joy,
Was their key to prosperity. Oh, boy –
Visit Blackburn! Its very existence
Was based on cotton. Now think 'subsistence'.
One mill, built for a hundred thousand pounds,
Was up for auction (including the grounds),
With no reserve – and not a single bid.
Priestley, again, is perfectly candid.
Nobody had any money to buy,
Rent or run a mill any more, that was why.

One "cotton king", his misery complete,
Was seen picking up fag ends in the street.
In the middle of the last century,
Its golden age, the cotton industry
Accounted for nearly thirty *per cent*
Of Britain's total exports. What this meant,
Of course, was that in Lancashire's heyday
The mill workers enjoyed fair rates of pay,

If never (surprise, surprise) excessive.
Their dwellings, though, were less than impressive,
Built in the shadow of the factories.

It is observations such as these,
By Priestley, that go some way to explain,
Once the work had disappeared down the drain,
Why people were left with slums to live in.
To build such hovels at all was a sin,
But deprive a worker of employment,
And all chances of good health, enjoyment
Of life, dignity, pride and self-respect
Disappear with it. What do men expect?
Some leadership, at least, in their affairs.
While politicians gave themselves airs,
The poor of Blackburn, neglected for years,
Suffered hunger, illness, trial and tears.

Rhyming History

To the Tyne, where Priestley explored Gateshead.
He approached the town with a sense of dread.
Mark this: it seemed to have been planned, this place,
"By an enemy of the human race" –
Some indictment – "*carefully* planned", to boot
(Priestley's words, my italics). Yet again,
Like Blackburn, a town under severe strain:
A place to work in; no place to live in;
Zero employment: an urban dustbin;
A money-making machine that had ceased
To make money. Sad, at the very least.
A scandal. The town had been left for dead.
No work, no industry: that was Gateshead.
One hundred and twenty-five thousand folk,
With nothing to do, no word of a joke.

Priestley, a compassionate sort of bloke,
Suggests any future historian –
Be their field modern or Victorian –
Should take a long, slow walk around Gateshead.
Sensible advice, it has to be said.
Only then should he or she deign to comment
On Britain's state of growth and development.

Down by the Quay, as far as he could go,
He saw many a dejected fellow,
Broken and miserable, down and out.
What hope did these men have? Little or nowt.
Slatternly women, gossips together,
Stood on their doorsteps, out in all weather,
Screaming at children playing in the dirt,
An outlook so depressing that it hurt.

T. S. Eliot wrote of a wasteland.
Priestley could have taken him by the hand
And shown him true devastation.
Behold the Tyne! Shame on the nation.

Depression and the Shadow of War

For this wasteland was hideously real.
"Industry had had a dirty black meal
"And had done no washing up." Down at heel,
And bleak, his next port of call was Jarrow,
Its mean streets monotonous and narrow,
Crammed with stunted, ugly houses. Sleep
Had been at a premium (you could weep)
For shipbuilding workers between shifts – so,
Barracks were erected where men could go
For food and rest. All were now derelict,
Fallen into disuse. Priestley's verdict?
"An idle and ruined town", Jarrow's poor,
"In the drawn masks of prisoners of war",
Condemned to the scrapheap for evermore.

Hebburn, if possible, was worse: distress,
Penury, "a fantastic wilderness
"Of decaying sheds" and "strange mounds and pits,
"Old concrete, iron twisted into bits,
"Fine big steamers rusting away in rows…"

This was Hebburn. As everyone knows,
In an age of shipbuilding mania,
Tyneside prospered. The *Mauretania*,
The famous liner, was launched at Wallsend,
Across the river from Jarrow. Her end,
Alas, was in sight (scrapped in '35),
But she was built when Tyneside was alive.
Now Jarrow was abandoned, and Hebburn,
Dead in the water, was no one's concern.

Yet the countryside around Wearsdale,
Its hills and streams, and the glens of Teesdale,
Comprising West Durham, was beautiful –
As fine as East Durham was pitiful.
For that was a poor coal-mining district.
As such, nobody bothered to visit.

Rhyming History

It is no coincidence (or is it?)
That there are no pits in or near London.
If there were, history (all said and done)
Would have to be rewritten. Rather fun:
A radical change. Why? No mystery.
Awareness of the mining industry,
Its pain and its pitfalls (literally),
Would challenge the complacent attitudes
Of the politicians. Platitudes?
No longer! With mines in their own backyard,
Even the most dyed-in-the-wool blackguard,
The most blinkered Tory, would struggle hard
To deny the miner a living wage
And safer conditions. Disengage?
Not an option. Complete ignorance
Is always easier at a distance.

Priestley makes a good point. Who, on the whole,
Knows (or wants to) anything about coal?
How many Members of Parliament,
He asks, could make a well-informed comment
On the life of a miner? Come to that,
How many voters? And I'll eat my hat
If newspaper editors knew, or cared,
About coal. Priestley agreed. He despaired,
But confessed that he too, up to a point,
Had ducked the issue. Loth to disappoint,
He took a detour, off the beaten track,
To East Durham. He was taken aback.

Seaham Harbour, a colliery town,
On the coast, was more destitute, run down
And dingy than he could have expected.
Few (when in work) earned more, he suspected,
Than thirty shillings a week – very low,
But the kind of statistic you should know.

Depression and the Shadow of War

What a town! His way with words never fails:
"It looks as weird as a cart-horse with scales
"And fins" – like no other he'd ever seen.
Dull, depressing, monotonous and mean,
Remote and dreary. What a place to live!

The cottages were small – "diminutive"
Is the word he uses, as if "playing,
"In a miserable way, at being
"A town": a monument to ugliness.

Here are some figures (I have to confess
My earlier ignorance): it appears
That 5,000 men died* in the five years,
To 1931, in accidents
Down the mines and, in other 'incidents',
Many thousands were injured – up to one,
Priestley reckons, in five. Ask anyone
In Seaham Harbour. Life was not much fun.

To make his visit to the town complete,
Priestley offers an arresting conceit.
During the War there was conscription.
What if a similar prescription

---

*A calculation in this regard,
According to the record in *Hansard*,
Bears this out: 800 fatalities
Over a span of ten months, if you please,
In 1930. Figures such as these
Are horrifying. As for injuries,
The numbers I've unearthed are less precise,
A surprise, nonetheless, and far from nice:
150,000, per year,
In non-fatal pit accidents, I fear.

Rhyming History

Was applied to the pits? The rates of pay
Would be broadly the same, that is to say,
At the very most, eight shillings a day.
Every man would have to work his share,
Whether he hailed from Billingsgate, Mayfair
Or the Isle of Dogs – indeed, anywhere.
"What a glorious shindy there would be,"
Writes Priestley, barely concealing his glee.
And if rich people could buy themselves out,
The wages would rise, no shadow of doubt.
A splendid idea! Why not try it?
The answer, I fear (and why deny it?):
The powers-that-be would never buy it.

We'll end our tour in Stockton-on-Tees,
Formerly prosperous, now on its knees.
Better looking than its larger neighbour,
Town of "beer and football", Middlesborough –
"More like a vast dingy conjuring trick"
Than a town – what made Stockton-on-Tees tick
Was shipbuilding. The year before the War
(1913), Britain built ships galore,
An output of some two million tons.
You wanted a ship? The Brits were the ones.

Nine tenths of the industry (this is true)
Had totally vanished by '32.
The consequence? Towns like Stockton-on-Tees
Hit the buffers. For places such as these
Knew only shipbuilding. Once in decline,
There was nothing. Coventry built cars, fine,
But to build motor cars in a shipyard?
Impossible. Times in Stockton were hard.

People had lost their jobs, their self-respect,
Their future prospects. What did they expect?

Well, more than they were given, that's for sure.
The workers of Stockton, the long-term poor,
Were offered nothing but more poverty.

"We can say *Shut Sesame*," writes Priestley,
With regret, 'but not *Open Sesame.*"
It's simple to shut down an industry;
To open a new one, not so easy.
We all bear some responsibility
For the neglect. Had London, to a man,
Been unemployed, they'd have soon found a plan.

Hats off to Priestley! You know I'm a fan.
Over the weeks since his journey began,
He has shown us England, warts and all –
Much to admire, but more to appal.

George Orwell and Walter Greenwood

A couple of books before we are done.
A George Orwell classic, second to none,
Is *Down and Out in Paris and London.*
This is Orwell's direct experience
Of real poverty. He sought to make sense
Of the downtrodden and the dispossessed.
The result? A book of the very best.
The clue is in the title! Have no doubt,
You'll feel what it's like to be down and out:
The dirt, the bed bugs, the ignominy,
The daily grind of abject poverty –
Above all else, the loss of dignity.

One work of fiction of the period
Is *Love on the Dole*, by Walter Greenwood.
Highly recommended, it's very good.
An uplifting story (in an odd way),
The domestic background, I'm sad to say,
Is bleak. Romance on a penny a day,
Or less, is certainly no holiday.
A loving couple, struggling, at best,
On next to nothing; the dreaded means test;
A family at odds; no one to blame,
Yet all overwhelmed with a sense of shame…
A spirit of true courage, in the end,
Carries the day. Soft-hearted? No. A blend
Of optimism, romance and sheer grit
Wins through. That's about the measure of it.

The 'Roaring Twenties'

The lot of the unemployed, and the poor,
Was desperate. Examples by the score
I could offer you. I shall say no more.
Yet, in the aftermath of the Great War,

There were many (those who could afford it)
Who craved pleasure. Not that I applaud it –
Given the terrible plight of the poor
In a world that was rotten to the core –
But, for those in work, living standards rose.
It is understandable, I suppose,
That they relished the opportunity
To pursue lives of increased gaiety,
Fun, laughter, irresponsibility
And indulgence. You have heard, I dare say,
Of the 'Roaring Twenties'. Well, these were they.

Night clubs and dancing

It was the craze for dance that set the tone.
There was no particular style alone
That led the field, but jazz, from the US,
A potent force, inspired its success.

Rhyming History

London was already familiar
With the Foxtrot and (not dissimilar)
The Tango – but others came thick and fast:
The Black Bottom (moralists were aghast)
And the Charleston. The worthy *Daily Mail*
Could always be relied on, without fail,
To denounce such imports: "reminiscent
"Only of Negro orgies". Innocent?
Of course! As were the night clubs and dance halls
That hosted them. The *Mail*'s rebuke appals.
What did it expect? Society balls?
Yet these 'dens of vice' had all the moralists,
And furious clergy, shaking their fists.

The Home Secretary entered the lists –
Sir William Joynson-Hicks (what a name!
You couldn't make it up), whose claim to fame
Was to denounce the night clubs as "a blot
"On the life of London". Like it or not,
There was little he could do. His powers,
Limited to the licensing hours,
Were insufficient to stem the tide.
Nonetheless, moralists were horrified
By the fact that by 1925
10,000 night clubs were known to thrive
In London alone. Even in the sticks –
Doubtless to the disgust of Joynson-Hicks –
Regular dances were held, if you please,
In halls up and down the land. What a wheeze!

Even the BBC, in '26 –
Reith, it seems, was a peculiar mix –
Had its own London Radio Dance Band,
An outstanding success, I understand.
Only six days a week: Sundays were out,
Reserved for the prim and ultra-devout.

'Flappers' and fashion

As fashion renounced the flounce and the frill,
The young took up the challenge with a will.

Hemlines were lifted (a bit of a thrill),
And corsets abandoned (bosoms were flat –
What would Victoria have made of that?),
As waistlines magically disappeared.
This was exactly as Joynson-Hicks feared:
Women had suddenly turned into boys.

Slim hips, flat chests, no whalebone! Joy of joys!
It was in with the bead, out with the pearl.
Your liberated, 'twenties', good-time girl
Was a flapper (so-called). Life was a whirl.
"*Adore* the frock, darling! Give us a twirl!"

In the War, when a girl might have a job,
Long hair could be a menace. Hence the 'bob',
Followed, in time, with even less on top:
In 1926, the 'Eton crop'.
The blink of an eye, that is all it took,
A bit of a shock in anyone's book.
Women transformed! A completely new look!

Cinema

The craze for dancing went hand in hand
With a passion for film. Understand,
If you will, that cinema-going
Was a 'must'. Full to overflowing,
The Embassy, the Regal, or the Ritz,
The Gaumont or the Rex, were no fleapits,
But temples of luxury. Art Deco,
Most of them, these were the places to go.

Rhyming History

Alfred Hitchcock was set to make his name
By '26, his steady rise to fame
Beginning with *The Lodger*, then *Blackmail*.
His genius was never known to fail:
The Lady Vanishes, Jamaica Inn…
Master of suspense, and sharp as a pin.
Stars of the screen, such as Charlie Chaplin,
And Gracie Fields, had punters flooding in.
Well over twenty million a week
Attended the cinema at its peak.
You needn't look far for the reason why:
Prices were low, and the quality high.
The films were simply there to be enjoyed.

There were reduced rates for the unemployed,
And you could stay for hours: a newsreel,
A B-feature (with limited appeal,
But at least the place was warm), a cartoon,
Then the main attraction. All too soon,
The programme was over. Next afternoon,
You could go again. Cinema was a boon.

Literature and literacy

Moving forward, T. S. Eliot called
The thirties (you can tell he was appalled)
That "low, dishonest decade". He was wrong,
In my view, for the British were on song.

For a start, they were highly literate.
Disengaged from politics? Not a bit.
Newspaper sales, by 1939,
Topped ten million – hardly a decline.
In fact, sales rose by one hundred *per cent*,
Or more, in twenty years, an increment
That was a truly glowing testament

To a healthy and growing interest
In public affairs. Beaverbrook did best,
Selling over two million copies
Of his *Daily Express.* Figures like these
Were encouraging, even though, I fear,
His newspaper was a rag. Year on year,
Membership of public libraries, too,
By a massive multiple, grew and grew.

Penguin Books

There was a thirst for books. Everyone
Knows of that publishing phenomenon,
Penguin Books. These were launched by Allen Lane,
In July, '35. How to explain
His success? Quite simple. The books were cheap.
The literary *élite* (you could weep)
Swore the idea would never catch on.

In four years, Lane was worth a million.
W. H. Smith had refused, at first,
To stock Penguins, snobbery at its worst.
Authors were fearful for their livelihoods,
If booksellers traded in 'shoddy' goods –
By which they meant 'cheap'. "Nobody can live
"Off sixpenny books," sniffed one. God forgive,
I say, such a short-sighted attitude.
Allen Lane accepted, with gratitude,
Woolworths' offer to take his books. Well done!
This set the trend. Seventeen million –
Yes, a huge number of Penguins – were sold
In under five years. It pays to be bold.

One of the first was Ernest Hemingway's
A Farewell to Arms. These were early days,
Too, for Agatha Christie's very first book.

Agatha Christie and crime

Allen Lane had taken an informed look
At *The Mysterious Affair at Styles*.
He was impressed. Agatha was all smiles.
Although first published in 1920,
Styles had earned Christie a pathetic fee.
Her *Murder on the Links,* similarly,
Had been bedevilled, unfortunately,
By its steep price and poor publicity.
This was where Allen Lane came in, you see.
Penguin proved a boon for Mrs. Christie,
And underpinned her popularity.

The earlier novels are among her best.
The Murder at the Vicarage passed the test,
In spades. But her most intriguing by far –
As the 'Queen of Crime' Christie raised the bar –
Was *The Murder of Roger Ackroyd*. Yes,
Mystery was the key to her success –
A wholesome 'whodunnit', no more, no less.

She beats other crime writers, I confess,
By a country mile. The major players –
The marvellous Dorothy L. Sayers,
Margery Allingham and Ngaio Marsh –
Cannot hold a candle to her. That's harsh,
I know. But as fictional sleuths go,
Who can match Miss Marple, Hercule Poirot,
Even Tommy and Tuppence, come to that?
Nobody I know, or I'll eat my hat.

John Buchan

The spy novel also came into vogue
Around this time Some contemptible rogue,

Russian (well, no Englishman at least),
Hell-bent on destroying Britain, the beast,
Would feature in Buchan, Somerset Maugham
Or Compton Mackenzie. Weather the storm,
And come out fighting – well, that was the gist.
The odd anarchist would never be missed!
Down with Johnny Foreigner! Quite a list,
In the case of John Buchan: *Huntingtower,*
The Thirty-Nine Steps (the man of the hour,
Richard Hannay) and *Castle Gay* are the best.

Popular novelists

The twenties and thirties were indeed blessed
With great story tellers: J. B. Priestley
(*Angel Pavement,* a favourite with me;
The Good Companions); Evelyn Waugh
(*A Handful of Dust; Vile Bodies* and more;
Scoop will have you in stitches, I am sure);
And the superb Daphne du Maurier –
See the film with Laurence Olivier,
Of *Rebecca; The Loving Spirit*, too;
Don't overlook, whatever else you do,
Jamaica Inn (these are only a few);
Then P. G. Wodehouse, crowning his career
With Jeeves and Wooster. Give them all a cheer.

D. H. Lawrence

We're in some danger of ignoring here
The more serious voices. There's James Joyce –
Sadly not my first novelist of choice;
And D. H. Lawrence. The latter, to me,
Is a true giant, the epitome
Of a great writer. He suffered, sadly,
From naked prejudice and bigotry.
The likes of our chum Joynson-Hicks, you see,

Loathed all things sexually explicit.
In the case of Lawrence, he had a fit.
The Rainbow had been impounded, and banned,
During the War. Not hard to understand,
Therefore, why its sequel, *Women in Love*,
Lawrence kept under wraps. Heavens above,
How narrow-minded could the censors be?

So, when it came to *Lady Chatterley*,
Lawrence hadn't a hope. No mystery,
I fear, why this fine novel was denounced.
"The foulest book," one stern critic announced,
"In English literature." "Sex-sodden,"
Lawrence was labelled. I call that rotten.
Chatterley was a "fetid masterpiece".
He fled abroad. He would never find peace
In Britain. A towering genius,
Lawrence was too good for the likes of us.

The continuing financial crisis

Meanwhile, how was the government faring –
The National Government? Daring?
Hardly. The run on the pound continued.
MacDonald dithered (I'm not being rude –
It's the only way it can be construed).
He worried now about the Gold Standard.
Snowden took the plunge (it must have been hard),
And the new government abandoned gold.
The revised strategy was hardly bold:
They were forced into it. Gold, you'll recall,
Had been seen as the be-all and end-all.
No longer. MacDonald was out of sorts,
But in order to save British exports
A devaluation of the pound –
Before it effectively hit the ground –
Of twenty-five *per cent* was accepted.

Cutting free of gold was unexpected.
Letting sterling sink to its own level
Had once been seen as the very devil.
A major sea-change occurred overnight.
What Britain now had to do was sit tight,
Manage the budget and weather the storm.
This was a watershed, far from the norm.
A new world of managed economies,
Planned budgets and free-floating currencies
Had fast become the order of the day.
That is my understanding, anyway.

A new mandate for the Tories

A stable majority was lacking
For the government. It wanted backing
From the people – to be blunt, a mandate.
The electorate would decide its fate,
October the 27th the date.
Its 'manifesto' had a phoney ring:
The Cabinet could agree on nothing,
Except the prevailing necessity
Of saving the ailing economy.
The Tories favoured protection. Well,
The Liberals (Snowden too, truth to tell)
Were strongly opposed. So, the argument
Was hushed up. The government was hell-bent
On defeating Labour. That was enough.
Snowden denounced their programme (stirring stuff),
To his shame, as "Bolshevism run mad" –
These his former colleagues. Dreadfully sad.

The strategy worked. Labour had run away:
Such was the verdict on election day.
Ramsay MacDonald appealed for unity.
Baldwin's Tories seized the opportunity

Of speaking up for Britain (it never fails),
While the Liberals limped in on their coattails.
The result? Labour, with one third of the vote,
Held just fifty-two seats. Never one to gloat,
MacDonald expressed some measure of regret.
The Tories' tally was their most stunning yet:
Some four hundred and seventy-three seats won –
A resounding victory, all said and done;
National Liberals took thirty-five,
A pathetic score, in their bid to survive.
While National Labour (MacDonald's wee band)
Managed thirteen. It's important to understand,
However, that it was Ramsay's triumph too.
Baldwin's Tories needed him, and this he knew.

It was one of politics' oddest stories:
A re-elected Commons stiff with Tories,
Yet led by a Prime Minister whose party
Had won a mere handful of seats. Bluff, hearty,
And outwardly relaxed, Baldwin was content
To accept the result, as far as it went.
Second-in-command, he'd fallen on his feet,
For Stanley was firmly in the driving seat.

Chancellor of the Exchequer Chamberlain

Or was he? It was Neville Chamberlain
Who would dominate, rather than Baldwin.
Chamberlain had replaced Philip Snowden
At the Exchequer. More than anyone,
Chamberlain was a protectionist.
Snowden, to be honest, was not much missed:
As Lord Privy Seal, in the House of Lords,
The comfort that the Upper House affords
Was now his. In September '32,
The ex-Chancellor caused quite a to-do.

Depression and the Shadow of War

He resigned from office altogether.
The improving economic weather –
Though unemployment was still appalling –
Must have seemed particularly galling,
Overseen, as it was, by a Tory.

Be that as it may, the end was gory.
He loathed protection. He'd had enough.
End of Snowden. He walked off in a huff.

Chamberlain set to work, in '32,   **1932**
With a will. The very least he could do
Was impose a tariff of ten *per cent*
On all imports (although, for the present,
Not on goods from within the Empire).
On some the duty was even higher:
Luxury goods at twenty-five *per cent*,
And over thirty (more than was decent)
On chemicals, bicycles and spare parts.

The move to tariffs gladdened Tory hearts.
It heralded the most hopeful of starts.
These changes apart, there was little new
In Neville's first budget. Savings were few,
Though estimates for arms production
Were low, leading to a reduction
In defence capability. Oh, dear:
Chamberlain would later argue, we hear,
For increased armaments expenditure,
Which was then accepted without demur.

Chamberlain was renowned for his *hauteur*,
An unclubbable old fellow. Narrow,
In his views, yet as straight as an arrow,
Focused, robust, hard-working and honest,
Neville stood head and shoulders, no contest,

Rhyming History

Above his colleagues. He got in a mess
Over Munich, a source of bitterness,
The mother of all disasters, no less –
"Peace in our time!" That's for later. For now,
Neville Chamberlain called the shots, and how.

"Weaned on a pickle!" That's some epitaph,
He found it hard to enjoy a good laugh.

Yet he triumphed as Chancellor, not half.
The country was in need of a cold bath,
And the country got it. I shall be brief.
Empire Free Trade (his dream) came to grief:
None of the Dominions would wear it.
Chamberlain was forced to grin and bear it.
Rather than 'imperial preference',
Minding their own backs made absolute sense.
Other protective measures, in essence,
Dictated Dominion policy –
And who could blame them, in all honesty?

A mere blip, this was quickly forgotten.
What Chamberlain did do (which was rotten)
Was reduce direct taxes to favour
The better-off. To offer a flavour,
Some two thirds of government revenue
Came from direct taxes in '32;
However, by the time Neville was through,
He'd brought it down to fifty-five *per cent*.
This figure was quite without precedent:
Over four fifths the ratio had been
When the War ended in 1918.
The consequent injustice was obscene:
A poor man on one hundred pounds a year
Ended up paying twice as much, I fear,
As a proportion of his income,
As one on five hundred. All right for some.

Depression and the Shadow of War

Indirect taxation was less fair,
By far, than direct. Why should Neville care?
Government funds had to come from somewhere.
What a man took home was his own affair.
The rich and the relatively well off
Prospered – the successful tradesman, the toff,
The man of business, the middle class –
While the poor suffered. A sickening farce.
Those very same people, without a doubt,
Had voted in droves to keep Labour out.
They now enjoyed their reward. Chamberlain
Was thanking his troops for the Tory win.

On the other hand, to Neville's credit –
He deserves some applause; there, I've said it –
He converted the rate of interest
On War Loan, in his unremitting quest
For solvency, to three-point-five *per cent*,
From five. This made a significant dent
In the deficit, given that the fund
Stood at two billion. Savers were stunned,
But the consequent benefit, we hear,
To the government finances, per year,
Was over eighty-six million pounds.
Complacent? Chamberlain had ample grounds.
For these bondholders were the very folk
Who'd voted him in, no word of a joke.

So the Chancellor, in adverse weather,
Contrived to put two and two together
And make five. Hence his claim, in '34,
That "the story of *Bleak House*" was no more,
And that the country could now look forward –
Provided nothing happened untoward –
"To *Great Expectations*". Fall on his sword?
Never. For Chamberlain was a success.

A steadily improving economy

The economy made steady progress,
Though whether by luck (my personal guess)
Or judgement, who can tell? By '33,   **1933**
At the latest, Britain's economy
Was turning the corner. Recovery,
Albeit arduous, halting and slow,
Was beginning. For five years in a row,
Productivity rose by six *per cent*,
Year on year, hardly insignificant.

Even employment, as far as it went,
Showed a steady, if modest, improvement:
By '37, ten *per cent* higher
Than in '32 – much to admire,
Though when reflecting on unemployment,
Nationwide, think what the numbers meant.

North and South

The statistics for 1934
Are shocking. For Jarrow (this I deplore),
The mean percentage unemployment rate
Was a massive sixty-seven-point-eight.
In Oxford, we read, it was five-point-one.

A scandal. Southerners basked in the sun,
While life on the Wear, all said and done,
Was little better than death, utter grind,
Hell on earth. The north had been left behind.

Britain's pressing economic crisis
Helps explain the government's emphasis
On finance. They were taken unawares
By a gathering storm: foreign affairs.

Weakness of the League of Nations

Complacency was the name of the game.
The relentless arms race was held to blame,
In retrospect, for the outbreak of war,
In 1914. The answer, therefore,
To future conflicts was disarmament.
The League of Nations was quite content,
Through negotiating machinery,
To offer a 'collective' guarantee
For world peace – a form of security
To prevent wars breaking out by mistake
(As in '14). What an error to make!

Manchuria

The League's 'powers' were merely persuasive.
If this seems spiritless and evasive,
It was. The big test came in '31.
I am sad to say that little was done
When Japan sent an invasion force
Into Manchuria. The League, of course,
Did nothing. A Chinese province? Who cared?
Drive out the Japanese? Nobody dared.
It wasn't that no one bothered at all,
They simply did not have the wherewithal,
Not least the British. For we had wound down
Our troops: they'd have run us out of town.
Anyway, force exceeded the League's brief –
Which is why Japan, like a common thief,
Was permitted to get away with it.
Palmerston, methinks, would have had a fit.

The British urged conciliation.
Big deal! Japan, a member nation
Of the League (it's true), could not have cared less,
When the Chinese government sought redress.
The whole fiasco was rather a mess.
It served to lower the League, for certain,
In the eyes of the world. Coercion?
Forget it. There was an aversion,
Clearly, to any kind of action.

So what was MacDonald's reaction
To the invasion? "Wicked," he said.
Ramsay might just as well have stayed in bed.
As for sanctions: not even mooted.
Peace and the League were very ill suited.
When an inquiry under Lord Lytton
Wrote its Report (was there ever written

A more pusillanimous document?),
It sided with Japan, to some extent,
Though it did condemn the invasion.
The Japanese used the occasion
To leave the League: yes, for throughout all this
She had remained a member. Cowardice,
Timidity, weakness and lack of will…
The shame of the incident haunts us still.

Disarmament

Despite Manchuria, despite Japan,
The government was resolved, to a man,
To press on with disarmament, the key
To peace in Europe. Rearm? Not likely.
Foreign wars were caused by "great armaments": *
Disarmament, therefore, made perfect sense.
Ever reluctant to sit on the fence,
MacDonald resolved to stick with his plan.

The Disarmament Conference began,
Convened in Geneva in '32.
The stakes were high and this MacDonald knew.
He ignored Japan (what else could he do?)
And kept on going. The difficulty
Was the rift between France and Germany,
Over the issue of arms parity.
The French had fears for their security,
Should the Germans achieve equality.
The British sought to encourage the French,
Either to disarm (a terrible wrench)

---

*This was David Lloyd George's professed view
(The phrase was his) and that of others too.

To a level equal with Germany –
MacDonald argued this most earnestly –
Or to allow the Germans to rearm
Up to the French level. Where was the harm,
Asked the PM? Conciliation,
Vastly better than confrontation,
Was the only way forward. Not for France!
Weary of this old diplomatic dance,
She refused to budge. The result? Deadlock.
Disarmament took a near-fatal knock.

The rapid rise of Hitler

Germany then caused an almighty shock.
On the 30th of January,
The following year, 1933,
Adolf Hitler became her Chancellor –
Or the Nazis moved in, if you prefer.

Hitler worked fast (don't tell me you're surprised),
More rapidly than many realised.
He seized dictatorial powers: yes,
Within the space of two months. It's my guess –
And that of many others, I confess –
That the burning down, in February,
Of the *Reichstag* was no conspiracy
(As alleged) by the dreaded Communists,
But a Nazi plot. The Nationalists,
Hitler's surprise allies, suffered a hit,
When dubious sources blamed them for it,
But this was Hitler's handiwork, no doubt.
It was Nazi thugs who carried it out.

For the Germans this was serious news.
A dictatorship, whatever their views,
Was a slippery slope. As for the Jews,

Their persecution quickly began.
Hitler's opponents, according to plan,
Were 'liquidated'. It was plain to see.

The leadership of the Nazi Party,
In June '34, was purged. 'Moderates',
Thought to be Hitler's close associates,
But reckoned not to be loyal enough,
Were murdered in the night. Frightening stuff.
More than two hundred others lost their lives,
Shot in broad daylight. The record survives.

There were concentration camps for Jews,
Gays, gypsies and more. Stiffen the sinews?
Rearm? Brace ourselves against the threat?
Britain was loth to do anything yet.

Rhyming History

Pacifist sentiment

Politicians were aware, you bet,
Of what was going on. The full extent?
Perhaps not. But MacDonald was hell-bent,
Still, as were others, on disarmament.
Ramsay was a reasonable fella,
But faced an impossible dilemma.

Adolf Hitler was unreliable –
This was already undeniable –
An ogre and an aberration,
But war was beyond contemplation.
So, press on with negotiation,
That was the only option. Give in?
No. For there was still a battle to win,
And that had to be by disarmament.

One has to sympathise, in the event,
With Ramsay MacDonald. With all his heart
He yearned for peace. He'd made a decent start,
But things were beginning to fall apart.

He was not alone. Oh, by no means no!
The Oxford Union (maybe you know)
Voted, in February '33,
That it would "fight for its King and Country…
"In no circumstances", more's the pity.
A loyal one hundred and thirty-three
Voted against, but the majority,
Two hundred and seventy-five, said "aye!" –
Pacifist sentiment was running high.

This trend was confirmed later in the year,
At the Fulham by-election. Here,
To some surprise, the Tory candidate
Lost a majority (such was his fate)

Of over fourteen thousand to Labour.
They won a majority to savour:
Some four thousand, eight hundred and forty.
The unfortunate defeated Tory
Had been happy to go to any length
To argue than an increase in the strength
Of the armed forces was essential.
For Labour this was providential:
The Tories, they chorused, were all for war!
The facts were twisted, and this I deplore,
But politics are dirty, after all.

Fulham was more than a mere party brawl.
Stanley Baldwin stood appalled. "A nightmare,"
He called it, in a rare show of despair.
There was little now that Baldwin could do,
In the light of the 'pacifist issue',
But eschew rearmament. Take a lead?
Not his style. Take a risk? Surely no need.

The Nazis

Besides, National Socialism
In Hitler's Germany (*viz.* Nazism)
Was preferable to Communism,
Thought the Tories. Hitler was here to stay,
So we'd better accept it, come what may.
He was Germany's problem anyway.

This was a dangerous illusion.
All was thrown into confusion
When, in October, Nazi Germany,
Suddenly and unilaterally,
Turned her back on the League of Nations.
The serious strain on relations,
Within Europe, that her withdrawal caused
Was a severe blow. Even Baldwin paused,

And MacDonald – he in particular,
For simultaneously Herr Hitler
Put paid to Mac's hopes of disarmament,
By leaving the Conference too. This meant,
In effect, that the policy was dead.
The country would have to rearm instead.

Der Führer

The picture grew more grim by the hour,   **1934**
As Hitler strengthened his grip on power.
The German President Hindenburg died,
In '34. They were quick to decide
(The Nazis) that the roles of Chancellor
And President should be merged: *der Führer*
They called him. Step forward, Adolf Hitler.

German rearmament

Germany, Churchill warned, was "arming fast".
Winston, in the wilderness, was aghast
At British complacency. Now, at last,
The people would sit up and take notice.
In November he warned the House of this:
Within the space of a year, Germany,
For sure, would have achieved air parity
With Britain. By 1937,
He predicted, the Nazis, great Heaven,
Would have built up an air force twice as large.

Stanley Baldwin flatly denied the charge.
Churchill was wide of the mark. In the air,
The British were strong – no need to despair.
Germany's strength was half that of Britain,
And in a year's time the country's margin
Would still be greater by fifty *per cent.*

Baldwin's reassurances were well meant,
But in '35, the following May,
He had to retract, I'm sorry to say.

Defence

The defence estimates, for '34,
Were lower than for the ten years before,
Despite these warnings. Should there be a war,
Britain was lamentably ill-prepared.
It's as if the government hardly dared
To heed the danger. As Churchill despaired,
The powers-that-be, their heads in the sand,
Blundered on. It is hard to understand,
Looking back, how they could have done nothing.
Hindsight, of course, is a wonderful thing.

The Chiefs of Staff were going up the wall.   **1935**
They did not agree with Baldwin at all,
Nor MacDonald. Something would have to give.
So they took a rare initiative.
Civil servants published a White Paper,
A definitive policy-shaper,
A bold *Statement Relating to Defence*.
Given the climate, it made perfect sense.
Issued on the 4th of March, '35,
It argued that, were Britain to survive,
She would need to be reliant on force.

The thunderbolt stuck in the throat, of course,
Of the Prime Minister. MacDonald knew,
And had always argued (one of the few)
That in the event disarmament failed –
Note: the talks had already been derailed –
War would be inevitable. So he,
Ramsay himself (who knew how willingly?),
Initialled the document: J. R. M.
The combined services chiefs (good for them)
Had given government a rude surprise.
It "could no longer," they said, "close its eyes
"To the fact that adequate defences"
Were "still required". So, mend your fences,
That's what the military experts meant –
And, from that moment on, rearmament
Became the policy of government.

The 'Peace Ballot'

Or was it? An informal 'Peace Ballot',
Of eleven million (that's a lot),
Conducted by volunteers, *ad hoc*,
Encouraged the government to take stock.
The survey was a most thorough process,
Asking straight questions, no more, no less.

Ought Great Britain to stay in the League? "Yes."
Were folk in favour (I have to confess,
These words were loaded) of disarmament
"By international agreement?"
"Yes." And were people for prohibiting
"Private arms manufacture?" "Yes." The sting,
For some, came in the final question,
Asked without the slightest suggestion
Of bias. Where one country has abused
(Attacked) another, should "measures" be used –
"Economic and non-military" –
Or, failing those, and if necessary,
"Military measures"? Those who said "yes"
To the first half (and the figures impress)
Numbered ten million, though rather less
To the second. Only sixty *per cent*
Said "yes", and those who expressed discontent
Numbered over two million. Those "noes",
Twenty *per cent* (pacific so-and-so's) –
And the two million more who abstained –
Gave licence to Baldwin to feel restrained
In his policy of disarmament.
For the new PM this was Heaven-sent.

Ramsay MacDonald's decline

Forgive me, for I've been running ahead.
MacDonald had resigned, I should have said.

To be blunt, his time had long expired.
A disappointed man, he was tired,
And in declining health. Aged sixty-eight,
All agreed he had left it very late
To step aside (many a PM's fate).
The poor fellow was visibly ailing.
Unable to sleep, his eyesight failing,

Mac was at risk of becoming a joke.
A sensitive, shy and well-mannered bloke,
His physical collapse was sad to see.
He was 'ramshackle Mac' – yes, really.
He suffered the acute embarrassment
Of losing his thread in Parliament.
It was time to go. This he told the King.

The King's Silver Jubilee

George would not contemplate him retiring
Before his Silver Jubilee, in May –
The 6th, a national holiday.
Ramsay MacDonald, believe it or not,
Was his favourite PM. The high spot,
For MacDonald, of the King's Jubilee,
Was his appearance, with the family,
On the Buckingham Palace balcony.
This was at the King's invitation.
He would never forget the ovation
That George received from a grateful nation.

The Jubilee was a sensation,
A national celebration
In tribute to King George the Fifth, the man.
It seemed that everyone was a fan.
George, a genuinely popular King,
Had proved firm of purpose and unchanging.
As other monarchies were tottering,
Britain's remained strong. Honour, dignity,
Decency – no King showed these more than he.

For George, his people were his family.
He had won their respect and loyalty,
Sharing their woes in times of peace and war.
He understood what monarchy was for.

On the evening of the 6th of May,
"At the close of this memorable day",
He broadcast to his people. "I thank you" –
And here he was speaking for the Queen too –
"For all the loyalty and, may I say,
"The love" (yes, indeed, love) "with which this day
"And always you have surrounded us."
A devout man, never one to fuss,
The King dedicated himself "anew
"To your service". This was honest and true.
He would keep his word. This the people knew.

There was one 'constitutional' lapse.
The Irish, not the most loyal of chaps –
Not that it really mattered, perhaps –
Boycotted the proceedings. Well, who cared?
MacDonald, for one. He wondered they dared.

A worthy and fair-minded sort of chap,
He deeply deplored their absence. "The gap,"
He wrote, "lay like a shadow of smallness
"Over a ceremony of bigness" –
An odd choice of words – "and graciousness."

Baldwin Prime Minister for the third time

So MacDonald, not a moment too soon,
Handed over, on the 7th of June,
To Stanley Baldwin. The latter's tribute
To his government colleague was a beaut:
He praised the old man for his loyalty,
Kindness, moral courage and courtesy.
He mentioned his physical courage, too.
Those who regretted his exit were few.
All in all he had not done that badly,
But he'd long outstayed his welcome, sadly.

He took Baldwin's place as Lord President.
It was Ramsay MacDonald's fixed intent
To keep the image of the government
As truly 'National'. This, of course,
Was a mere illusion. A spent force,
He feared, perhaps, the pain and emptiness
Of retirement. Sidelined, to his distress,
In Cabinet, he should have settled for less.

This was Stanley Baldwin's third, and last, stab
At the top job. His was no power grab.
Baldwin was well-liked and well-respected,
Not least by George, who clearly expected
A smooth and natural transition.
He assumed that Baldwin's position
Was that of successor. The irony
Is that solid, reliable Stanley

Was younger by little less than a year
Than MacDonald and his fitness, I fear,
Was doubtful. He was nearly sixty-eight,
A martyr to his nerves and overweight.
What was the first thing Baldwin told the King?
He needed two months' rest. Now, there's a thing!

Baldwin's inheritance was alarming.
Hitler's Germany, far from disarming
(Some hope), had, by the end of '34,
300,000 men, probably more,
In her army. The Treaty of Versailles
Had been careful, in terms, to specify
100,000, maximum. Nice try!
Hitler rode roughshod over the Treaty.
He also took the opportunity,
In clear contravention of the pact,
To introduce conscription. This act,
He claimed, had been rendered necessary
By the contents (any excuse, you see)
Of the White Paper, mentioned above,
On defence. Hitler, when push came to shove,
Would stop at nothing to impose his will.
Nazi Germany: a most bitter pill.

Abyssinia

Meanwhile, something distinctly sinister
Was happening in Abyssinia.
To put it in a nutshell, Italy,
Under one Benito Mussolini,
Had her eye on that downtrodden country.
"Warfare is to men as maternity
"Is to women." What a philosophy!
Indeed, it is difficult to conceive
Of a worse dogma. "I do not believe

Rhyming History

"In perpetual peace." The old story:
The prestige of military glory
Mussolini sought. The end was gory.

On October the 3rd, after, alas,
A campaign of bombing with poison gas,
The dictator launched his invasion
Of Abyssinia.* The occasion
Was ripe for military action,
But Britain, in hock to the peace faction,
Offered nothing. The result was a rout.

Politicians were riddled with doubt.
No one appeared to have the slightest clue.
Sanctions, probably, would have to do…
Yet even here there was a reluctance
To upset Italy. Baldwin, for once,
Took a lead. But an oil embargo?
The French were hesitant to stop the flow:
Mussolini would be livid, so no!
Since all three countries faced a common foe,
Nazi Germany, they thought it unwise
To alienate possible allies.
Though Mussolini had sprung a surprise

---

*Strictly speaking, this is a misnomer.
The country's name was Ethiopia,
Abyssinia simply a province.
The error has been corrected long since:
Ethiopia it is called today.
'Abyssinia', however, held sway
In common parlance, so that's what I'll use.
Given the custom, it's hard to refuse.
They all referred to Abyssinia –
The press, the public, the Prime Minister.

By taking Abyssinia by storm,
The pillars of the League (sadly the norm,
After Manchuria) sat on their hands.

Another election

Sanctions apart, Baldwin, one understands,
Decided he had bigger fish to fry.
What of Mussolini, I hear you cry?
Well, Abyssinia would have to wait.
The Prime Minister didn't hesitate…
To call an election. Yes, that's right –
For Stanley had his own campaign to fight.

Rhyming History

He sought a mandate for rearmament,
But his tone (Baldwin in his element)
Was cautious. The country's defences
Must be strengthened. We must mend our fences.
There could be no wavering, no weakness,
No uncertainty and no squeamishness:
"All we have and hold is in jeopardy" –
Simple "doubts as to our own safety"
Gave "no assurance of peace". Stirring stuff.

Persuasion was no longer enough,
Without the force of arms. He gave his word,
However (was anything so absurd?),
That "there would be no great armaments". Well,
What this commitment meant was hard to tell.

The Prime Minister's speech earned him high praise.
That's fine, if you want to have it both ways.
It certainly worked. The outcome was stark.
From the Conservatives' high watermark,
In '31, they suffered a decline,
But only minimal. Labour did fine,
Their seats numbering one hundred and two,
But still with too few members, far too few,
To have any impact on policy.

They had played a poor hand, quite honestly,
Still intent on "seeking security
"Not through rearmament" (Clement Attlee),
"But through disarmament". Baldwin, you see,
Had touched a nerve. National Labour
Were trounced. In a victory to savour,
Emanuel Shinwell was elected
At Seaham: MacDonald, as expected,
Went down to a sad and heavy defeat,
His disgrace (as Labour saw it) complete.

MacDonald's pain

This was the end indeed. The PM wrote,
"My heart is heavy for you" (a kind note),
As he offered his old colleague his hand
"In enduring friendship". To understand
MacDonald's pain was one thing, but to lose
His Lord President was unwelcome news.
The ex-PM's place, whatever one's views,
At the highest level of government
Was key. It was what 'National' meant.

The poll, however, as far as it went,
Was yet another triumph for Baldwin.
The Liberals continued in a spin,
Down from thirty-three last time to twenty,
The cause for angst and regrets aplenty.
Even these twenty were split. One faction,
To Lloyd George's patent satisfaction,
Was his family 'tribe'. They numbered four:
Goronwy Owen (a distant in-law),
His daughter Megan, and Gwilym, his son –
Proof, were any needed, his day was done.

The Hoare-Laval Pact

The urgent item in Baldwin's in-tray
Was Abyssinia. Fit for the fray?
Well… He hoped the problem would go away.
It didn't, of course. What more can I say?

The new (Tory) Foreign Secretary
Was Sir Samuel Hoare. He was wary
Of offending Mussolini. Scary.
He met with French PM Pierre Laval,
In secret (a sort of two-man cabal),

Rhyming History

In December, while on his holidays.
Their 'pact' was calculated to amaze:
The Hoare-Laval Pact it came to be called.
It was leaked. The British press were appalled,
Including *The Times*, proven Baldwin fans.

This was the gist of Sir Samuel's plans.
Territory to the north and south-east –
60,000 square miles of land at least –
Would be handed over to Italy.
Furthermore, the greed of Mussolini
Was to be assuaged by the outright grant
Of economic rights (my giddy aunt!)
Over the southern part of the country.

Abyssinia was up a gum tree.
The only notable concession made –
Little better than a sop, I'm afraid –
Was a corridor of land to the sea,
Granted, begrudgingly, by Italy.
This tract, dubbed by *The Times* (yes, really)
"A corridor for camels", says it all.

The Prime Minister and others could fall,
It was that serious. Sir Samuel
Hoped to secure the backing of Baldwin.
Stanley, fresh from his electoral win,
Was slow to come to terms with Hoare's mistake.

His colleagues were quicker on the uptake.
A flurry of resignation threats
Upset the balance. Few were placing bets
On Hoare's survival. Baldwin was surprised
By the uproar. He hadn't realised
The strength of feeling in Britain at large.
He had won his mandate. He was in charge.

…Or was he? A sell-out to Italy
Reflected badly (nay, pitifully)
On his assurances, in retrospect,
That the British, through the League, would respect
The rights of others. Austen Chamberlain,
Formerly a staunch ally of Baldwin,
Was horrified, and glad to have his say:
"Gentlemen do not behave in this way."

Hoare's dismissal

At first the PM sought to bluff it out,
But his lowest point, no shadow of doubt,
Was when he stood before Parliament
And made the following foolish statement:
Were the troubles over, he'd "make a case",
But all he could say for now (saving face?)
Was "my lips are not yet unsealed". What rot!

Baldwin thereafter became known, the clot,
By the nickname 'old sealed lips'. David Low,
The cartoonist, compounded Stanley's woe

By drawing him with a sticking plaster
Over his mouth. An utter disaster.

Baldwin could not get rid of Hoare faster.
Sir Samuel, bless his heart, was dismissed.
It's fair to say that he wasn't much missed.

The well-regarded Austen Chamberlain
Was offered foreign affairs, a win-win –
Or so he thought. Then Baldwin changed his mind.
Was this careless, planned, or simply unkind?
Austen was snubbed, but he never knew why.
He saw red. "Sly, sir, devilishly sly":
His chapter heading, he said, on Baldwin
Should he write a book! His besetting sin
(Stanley's) was ego. He was idle, too,
Ruthless to boot. So what did Baldwin do?
He offered the job to Eden, *in lieu*:
"It looks as if it will have to be you!"

The Hoare-Laval Pact was dead. However,   **1936**
Mussolini, so fiendishly clever,
Pressed on regardless. You can forget France.
The whole of Europe could see at a glance
That Laval was prepared to do nothing.

The death of the Pact was at least something,
But not enough. Events were moving fast.

Hitler's occupation of the Rhineland

The British and French alike were aghast
When Hitler re-occupied the Rhineland –
In breach of Versailles, you should understand.
The Rhineland was Germany's 'back garden',
And neither country had the strength (pardon?)

To stop her. So Stanley Baldwin confessed,
With tears in his eyes, he was that distressed.

Nor had either the will. This Hitler guessed.
There was regrettably no appetite
For action, no stomach for a fight.
Herr Hitler judged the mood exactly right.
The French could have attacked him with justice,
The truth of this too obvious to miss.
His generals fully expected this,
But Hitler overruled them. His success
Strengthened his hand. Had he settled for less,
He would not have been the man Europe feared.
No one could stop him, or so it appeared.

Haile Selassie into exile

Mussolini ploughed on with his campaign
To conquer Abyssinia. Again,
Dictatorship triumphed and won the day.
Hoare and Laval would have given away
Swathes of the country. Now, to the dismay,
And discomfort, of Haile Selassie
(The Emperor), a cool Mussolini
Invaded. He was to seize even more
Than the Pact had offered. This I deplore.

With menace, over the south-east border,
His armed regiments, well out of order,
Crossed from Italian Somaliland.
Selassie's forces, a pitiful band,
Were driven out. There were atrocities
On both sides – chemical casualties,
And evidence of torture, if you please,
Among the dead and wounded. Sad to say,
The Emperor, on the 2nd of May,
Was forced into exile. He fled to Bath.

Death of the League

With the Italians on the warpath,
He had little choice. Addis Ababa
Was taken by storm and (a bridge too far)
Italy's King Victor Emmanuel
Was named as Emperor. In a nutshell,
The dictator had got away with it.
Sanctions proved of little benefit.
They were dropped like a stone. The League was dead.
The future could only be faced with dread.

Opinions differ. It has been said,
Frequently, that if Britain had held out
Against Italy, and shown some clout
When it came to Hitler, then, beyond doubt,
We'd not have been given the runabout
In 1939. The Second World War?
Forget it. What were our armed forces for,
If not to face up to aggression?
Politics? A noble profession.
But to take the path of least resistance
Was pure folly. In the present instance,
Had France and Britain faced up, together,
To Italy, whatever the weather,
And to Germany in those early years,
We might have been spared the blood, sweat and tears
That were coming our way. Who is to know?
It is simply guesswork, so on we go.

Death of King George the Fifth

The King died in January, I fear,
1936. Three Kings in one year:
George, Edward the Eighth, then George, his brother,
A royal succession like no other.

Depression and the Shadow of War

King George delivered his final broadcast
At Christmas. Sadly, he was fading fast.
The entry in his diary (his last)
For the 17th of January
Records that he saw his doctor, briefly,
And "I feel rotten". The Queen was worried.
She summoned the Prince of Wales, who hurried
(By aeroplane) to Sandringham. The heir,
Two days later, motored to London. There,
With regret, he told Baldwin that the King,
The Emperor, his father, was dying.

The country was taken quite by surprise.
The King represented, in people's eyes,
All that was steady and reliable.
The truth of this was undeniable.
King George the Fifth stood as a noble rock
In a great sea of troubles. Profound shock,
And sorrow, his subjects suffered. The clock
Was ticking. The news on the BBC –
Read with appropriate solemnity –
Spoke of the King's life "moving peacefully
"Towards its close". His dying words, some say,
Were, "How is the Empire?" To this day,
There is a rumour (which I much prefer)
That he really said, "Bugger Bognor!"
The seaside resort had been suggested
By his doctor, a place George detested.

Whether these were his final words or not,
The legend lives on, and it says a lot
For his blunt manner – one reason, I feel,
For his strong, earthy, popular appeal.

On the twentieth, at five to midnight,
He died. Baldwin pitched it precisely right:

George had earned "the respect and loyalty"
Of all. He had shown that monarchy
Was proof against the kind of tyranny
That threatened Europe. In "our country"
It was as native "as oak or ash or thorn".
Was ever a more homely orator born
Than Baldwin? The King's coffin was taken
From Sandringham, if I'm not mistaken,
Attended by his beloved Charlotte.
A female relative? No, his parrot –
And Jock, the King's favourite white pony.

Could Edward emulate George? If only!
For now, he behaved to perfection.
His display of love and affection
Was genuine and surely not for show,
Though the King and his son had not been slow

To share their grievances. Edward's lifestyle
George deplored. The Prince considered futile
The King's dogged resistance to progress.
They were often a loggerheads, no less,
Much to Queen Mary's despair and distress.

"After I am dead," the King told Baldwin,
"The boy," he foresaw, would come to ruin
"Within twelve months." Well, I shall eat my hat
If it didn't happen sooner than that.

EDWARD THE EIGHTH (1936)

Mrs. Simpson, to my way of thinking,
Saved us from a pretty appalling King.
Wallis Simpson was an American,
Divorced, and married to another man,
Whom she would shortly sue for divorce too.

Now you might have imagined, mightn't you,
That the King would steer clear of Mrs. S.
It soon became clear he couldn't care less.
Edward was forty-one. He'd had affairs
Before this one (like many royal heirs),
But he was caught completely unawares
By the strength of political feeling
Against Wallis. It left the King reeling.

Stanley Baldwin was slow on the uptake.
The foreign newspapers, make no mistake,
Were full of it, but, believe it or not,
The British press were not saying a lot.
The people were in total ignorance
Of a crisis. Off to the south of France,
On a yacht, the King went on holiday,
With Mrs. Simpson. What more can I say?

Edward the Eighth's character

Wallis apart, there can be little doubt
That the new King would *not* have been forced out.
Edward was most unsuitable, it's true.
He was lazy and louche. Most people knew
(It was no secret) that he sympathised
With Hitler's Nazis. So few were surprised
That he failed to recognise the danger –
Or perhaps didn't care. Truth is stranger,
They say, than fiction. Who would have thought
That Edward the Eighth, an affable sort,
Might have brought down the British monarchy
Within twelve months? Baldwin (this we shall see)
Contrived to avert the catastrophe.

The Abdication crisis

For Stanley was focused and kept his cool.
He declined to force Edward's hand. No fool,
Baldwin acted with tact and vision:
The King must make his own decision.

And so he did. It was made clear to him
He had two choices. He was far from dim,
And he well understood the dilemma.
Edward, at heart a sensible fella,
Would have to give up the love of his life
Or renounce the throne. It cut like a knife,
But he chose Mrs. Simpson. There was talk,
Among friends, that, rather than take a walk,
A marriage could take place – 'morganatic',
So-called. The PM refused to panic:
That Mrs. Simpson should marry the King,
With no rights or privileges, nothing,
Was not on the cards, and he made that plain.
It didn't take Baldwin long to explain
How awkward this arrangement would have been –
Wallis Simpson his wife, but not his Queen!

Edward then kicked up a bit of a scene,
By proposing a radio broadcast
To the nation. Baldwin was aghast.
His colleagues were urging him to act fast,
But their siren voices went unheeded.
He gave Edward all the time he needed,
But vetoed the broadcast: unusual
(At best) and unconstitutional.

Support for the King was ebbing away.
His cause was not much helped, I'm bound to say,
By Mosley's Blackshirts (an unpleasant crowd)
Standing shoulder to shoulder, strong and proud,

With the Communists in Edward's support.
He attracted strange bedfellows, in short –
Including Churchill, the little smarty,
Who tried to form a so-called 'King's Party'.

Then Simpson said she'd call off her divorce
And give up the King. He refused, of course.
Edward was set on abdication.
Wallis had become a fixation.

The Instrument of Abdication

In full charge of the situation,
Baldwin presented to Parliament,
On December the 10th, the Instrument
Of Abdication the King had signed,
And Edward and Wallis were soon consigned
To history. The Prime Minister's speech,
It's generally reckoned, was a peach.

The evening of the following day,
The former King finally had his say.
He addressed the British people, at last,
In a short farewell radio broadcast.
The "burden of responsibility"
Had proved impossible, for such as he,
Without, he declared, "the help and support
"Of the woman I love". Edward had fought
(Or had he?) to keep his seat on the throne.
Nonetheless, in these "few words of my own",
He explained why, as he put it, he "quit".

Edward the Eighth was patently unfit
To be King. The long and the short of it
Was this: he lacked stamina, courage and grit.
Well, that's one view. I give the man credit
For sticking to his guns. There, I've said it.

He never sought office. That much is clear.
Yet he caused offence, and it cost him dear.
The pair were married the following year.
Self-imposed exile is never, I fear,
A merry prospect. The couple, I hear
(I hope), found happiness. Give them a cheer.

GEORGE THE SIXTH (1936 – 1952)

Edward's brother Albert was unprepared
For kingship. In truth, the poor man despaired.
'Bertie' was Albert's family nickname.
Upon his accession, George he became –
King George the Sixth. It sounds rather absurd,
But in the family circle Edward,
The ex-King, had been known as David!

Whatever his name, Britain was well rid
Of Edward the Eighth. Rampantly right-wing,
He professed, as we've seen, a strong liking –
Nay, admiration – for Hitler. Well,
Imagine had the Nazis cast their spell
Over the King of England! Who's to say
What a pickle we'd have been in today.

The new King's character

His younger brother was quite different.
The Duke of York was modest, diffident,
Reserved and lacking in self-confidence.
Although he rarely seemed to take offence,
He lived, as a boy, in Edward's shadow.
The Prince of Wales, as heirs apparent go,
Was a true paragon: intelligent,
Good-looking and mobbed wherever he went –
The archetypal royal golden boy.
Life was for living, and there to enjoy.

Rhyming History

Bertie, by contrast, retiring and shy,
Suffered from a stammer. The reason why
Is not hard to fathom. The gruff old King,
His father, was stern and overbearing.
He set the highest standards for his sons.
Edward would rebel. He stuck to his guns,
Refused to be moved and argued the toss.

This was far from how Bertie came across.
Quite content to slip into the background,
The peace and tranquillity that he found
Were of his own making. George was aghast
When his second son managed to come last
In his naval exams. The King was proud,
Nonetheless, when young Bertie was allowed
(Despite the danger) to serve his country,
A midshipman in the Royal Navy,
In the war, on HMS *Collingwood.*
He had little doubt the boy would come good.

And so he did. Bertie's naval career
Was cut short by illness. He found no cheer
At Cambridge, where he was sent for one year
To readjust to civilian life.
In 1923 he took to wife
Elizabeth Bowes-Lyon, quite a catch –
Scottish nobility, the perfect match.
Elizabeth gave Bertie confidence.
With her dogged, yet gentle, persistence,
His stammer was cured – with the help, it's true,
Of a speech therapist. His courage grew,
Along with his domestic happiness.
Glamour and glory? He couldn't care less.

So the Duke watched with increasing alarm
As Edward contrived to do lasting harm

To himself and to the country at large.
Once convinced that he'd be called to take charge,
As King, he broke down and cried like a child.

For a nervous man, sensitive and mild,
This was an awesome and terrible test.
Yet Bertie wrote that he would "do my best
"To clear up the inevitable mess"
Should the worst happen. He could do no less.

King George the Sixth wins respect

Never had a reign begun more badly,
Despite the crowd he found "cheering madly"
In London. "When D. and I said goodbye,"
He wrote, his brother looked him in the eye,

Then they kissed "and he bowed to me as King".
His words have a sad and sorrowful ring.
Inexperience, more than anything,
Was the new King George's abiding fear.
Yet he earned the confidence, year on year,
Of his good subjects. He had never seen
A state paper – never. He was that green.

He kept faith. The King's dedication
To duty impressed the whole nation.
He rescued (no exaggeration)
The monarchy from a lingering death,
Serving the country to his final breath.
He died aged fifty-six. He bore the strain
With honour. Edward's loss was Britain's gain.

Stanley Baldwin's complacency

Regretfully, we have to turn again
To politics. The Coronation,   **1937**
A breath of fresh air for the nation,
Was unable to conceal the crisis.
The rise of Hitler's Nazis (not nice, this)
Was unstoppable, or so it appeared.

Baldwin's complacency, as many feared
(Churchill included), had ever been such
That rearming didn't bother him much –
Despite his paying lip service to it
At election time. Baldwin blew it,
That's the truth. Even Chamberlain knew it.

A cautious Chancellor, Chamberlain
Nonetheless lost patience with Baldwin.
In the early years Neville resisted
Increased expenditure. He insisted

Depression and the Shadow of War

On economy, putting prudence first.
Let Hitler and Germany do their worst,
The reluctant Chancellor had no thirst
For excess spending. Now he changed his mind.

The new Prime Minister was flying blind
In foreign affairs. At the end of May
Baldwin retired. He'd opted to stay,
Following Edward's Abdication,
Until after the Coronation –
Much, I gather, to the frustration
Of Chamberlain, then waiting in the wings.

Neville Chamberlain: the new Prime Minister

Once in office, of all unlikely things,
Chamberlain turned his close attention
To rearmament. There was tension,
Still, between the need for economy
And the call to rearm. Priority,
However, was given, for the first time,
To defence. Reckless spending was a crime,
In his book, but in his final Budget,
In February, to give him credit,
Chamberlain pushed Baldwin to the limit
With plans to borrow (the figure astounds)
The sum of four hundred million pounds,
Over five years, to be spent on defence.

It was thus down to Chamberlain's good sense
That the country was at least half-ready,
In '39, for war. Baldwin, steady,
Popular and unimaginative,
Rarely looked ahead. Something had to give.
This Neville recognised. It makes me sick
That Chamberlain, lambasted for Munich

(And rightly so), is given no credit
For rearmament. There now, I've said it.

Increased spending on armaments

In retrospect, he should have done far more,
But nobody, remember, wanted war –
Not even Churchill. Arms production
"To the limit" was the instruction
After '38. From '37,
Spending on the RAF, great Heaven,
Increased to such an impressive extent
As to cause vociferous discontent
In the ranks of both Army and Navy.

Where Baldwin had been relaxed (nay, lazy),
Neville was clear what he needed to do.
The Battle of Britain, won by "the few",
Was a small triumph for Chamberlain too.
By then, though, he had only months to live
And the British people, slow to forgive,
Remembered Munich. "Peace for our time":
A grisly, nauseating pantomime.

Appeasement

This was all that can be said, I regret,
For Chamberlain. He would rearm, and yet
This policy was to go hand in hand
With appeasement. He failed to understand
That Hitler was not a man you could trust.
Others would be sacrificed, as needs must,
To the "bully of Europe", if this meant
Keeping the peace. So much for appeasement.
Chamberlain made it abundantly plain
That he sympathised with Germany's pain

Over Versailles. Hitler made a good case
For the Sudeten 'Germans'. A disgrace.

Though Neville professed to loathe Nazism,
He fell prey to anti-Semitism
In his own throwaway comments. "No doubt,"
He said (sentiments we could do without),
"Jews aren't a lovable people." I mean!
In or out of context, this is obscene.
Nazi persecution of the Jews
He viewed with distaste. But the less good news
Was that Germany's domestic concerns
Were their own business. The more one learns,
I'm sad to say, of Neville Chamberlain,
The less one warms to him. Stanley Baldwin,
At least, was a clubbable old fellow.

Chamberlain was brittle, far from mellow,
Vain and opinionated. He'd say
(No joke) "so long as I have my own way,
"I don't object to opposition".
Self-doubt? An idle imposition!
He would save his country. He was the man:
"I do not believe anyone else can."
You'll have gathered by now, I'm no great fan.

Nazi Germany

Chamberlain failed to take seriously
The growing threat of Nazi Germany.
Even as late as June, 1918,
Germany's collapse had been unforeseen,
Defeat accepted by only a few.
The people were stunned. So what did they do?
They found a scapegoat. Kaiser Wilhelm? No.
Although no longer the people's hero,

Rhyming History

He was still a victim. Germany's woe,
Her ruin, resulted (so now we know)
From Jewish-Bolshevik conspiracies.
'Stab-in-the-back' theories such as these
Took hold with ease. Hyper-inflation,
Twinned with the deep humiliation
Of Versailles, fuelled nationalism,
Disorder and political schism.
The world crisis in capitalism,
The great depression, in this regard
Hit Germany particularly hard.

Unemployment, increasing year on year,
Hunger and want, bred a climate of fear
That sowed deadly seeds in the fertile soil
Of people's hearts. It all came to the boil
With Adolf Hitler's Nazis. Desperate
For hope, and leadership, Germany's fate
Was sealed. The Nazi Party was on song.
Hitler and his henchmen could do no wrong.

They rounded up opponents: communists,
Bolsheviks, political journalists,
Writers, academics and scientists.
They burned books. Heine (the poet, a Jew)
Had written years earlier (sadly true):
"Where one burns books, there, eventually,
"One will burn people." They showed no pity,
No respect. Massive support they enjoyed
Among the legions of unemployed.
No surprise there. For they promised them bread.
The economy, meanwhile, forged ahead:
Rearmament, Europe's first motorways –
A great leap forward from the bad old days.
In the three years post-1933,
Numbers in work in Nazi Germany
Increased by over twenty-five *per cent.*

Hitler's popularity

The Führer was mobbed wherever he went.
At Hitler's massed rallies the atmosphere
Was hysterical. The message was clear:
The Nazis would prevail. Versailles was dead.
The people would follow where Hitler led.

Unions were outlawed. They turned the screws
On liberals. As for Germany's Jews,
The campaign immediately began
To drive them out. Hitler's ultimate plan
Was to rid Europe of the Jewish race.
Folk were well aware what was taking place.
Some encouraged it, a total disgrace.
Others turned a blind eye. They let it go.
But no one could pretend they did not know.
Where was the harm? Why not go with the flow?

Rhyming History

Hitler's racial and expansionist policies

In his political manifesto,
Mein Kampf, Hitler made it perfectly clear
That the German nation should adhere
To racial policies: like with like –
People of the same blood in the same Reich.
His vision of foreign policy,
Uniting Austria with Germany
(In spite of Versailles), was plainly spelt out.
His readership was left in little doubt
That Germany enjoyed a moral right
To neighbouring lands. The future was bright.
German couples (imagine their delight!)
Were obliged to purchase their own copy
Upon marriage. So, nothing sloppy,
Or random, in the way the people's blood
Was poisoned. *Mein Kampf* was hardly a dud.

Hitler's quest for *Lebensraum*, it would seem,
('Living space'), was far from an idle dream.
This was real. Eastern territories –
Poland, the Ukraine, countries such as these,
The lion's share of Russia, indeed –
Were in his sights. Ambition and greed
Gnawed at Hitler's heart, revenge and malice,
Hatred and envy: a poisoned chalice.

The overwhelming tragedy of this
Is still, years afterwards, easy to miss.
When German troops marched into the Rhineland –
In 1936, you understand –
Had Hitler been stopped, he would have withdrawn,
Thus attracting the ridicule and scorn
Of his people. Could he have recovered?
Who knows? We would doubtless have discovered.

But the world let the Germans march straight in:
For Hitler and the Nazis, a clear win.

The folly of Lord Halifax

For Britain and France their cardinal sin
Was lack of courage. They minded their backs,
That was the truth of it. Lord Halifax,
Later a weak Foreign Secretary,
Told Hitler to his face (reckless, very)
That the vexed questions of Austria,
Of Danzig and the 'Polish corridor'
(So-called), and of Czechoslovakia,
Could be settled, to give you a flavour
(I kid you not), in Germany's favour,
Provided there were (whatever this meant)
"No far-reaching disturbances". Hell-bent,
As he was, on the domination
Of Europe, Hitler's consolation,
When he heard these sentiments, knew no bounds.
Halifax's folly simply astounds.

Indeed, Adolf Hitler had ample grounds
For 'annexing' Austria – this the view
Of Chamberlain, and his ministers too.
Besides, there was little Britain could do.
The Führer (this the Prime Minister knew)
Considered union "imperative".

Chamberlain submitted. Live and let live:
Too slow to object; too quick to forgive.
Halifax had intimated, of course,
That provided Hitler did not use force
Any steps the dictator chose to take
Could well be overlooked. Make no mistake,
Hitler's Nazis took this as a green light.

The *Anschluss*

Austrians reacted with pure delight   **1938**
(Most of them, anyway) when Germany
'Invaded'. In 1918, with glee,
They'd voted, by a large majority,
For *Anschluss*, that is to say, unity.
They were frustrated. It was not to be.
The Versailles Treaty, in terms, forbade it.
The pro-German Austrians had had it.

No longer! A rare political *coup*
Hitler staged. Fulsome gratitude was due
To the Führer. They were thrilled, through and through,
By their long-delayed liberation.
Anschluss meant the incorporation
Into the greater German nation

Of Hitler's Austria, now a province.
The fertile ground had been prepared long since,
For most Austrians were German at heart.
The Führer had made a promising start.

Austria was the land of Hitler's birth.
This was 'his' Austria, for what it's worth.
Her place in the new Nazi Germany,
Now no less than a racing certainty,
Was all the more welcome. It sounds absurd,
But no one opposed him. Chamberlain heard,
We're told, the terrible news over lunch,
On the 12th of March. If he'd had a hunch,
The merest inkling, of what was in store,
It's highly unlikely (need I say more?)
That he'd have invited Herr Ribbentrop,
German Ambassador! Caught on the hop,
Old Neville was in a bit of a stew.
Churchill was lunching at Number Ten, too.
I ask you, what could poor Chamberlain do?

The embarrassment! Rising to the test –
Chamberlain at his inadequate best –
The Prime Minister made a strong protest
To Berlin. This was of no interest
To Hitler. Now that Austria was his,
It was none of Great Britain's business.

The Jew-baiting terror,* deeply shocking,
Was worse in Austria, if anything,
Than in Germany. That's saying something.
As usual, her neighbours did nothing.

The writing, however, was on the wall.
The *Anschluss*, calculated to appal,
Was just the beginning. This Churchill knew,
And he spoke up strongly, one of the few.

Rhyming History

The next target? Czechoslovakia.
Why should the Führer stop at Austria?

Czechoslovakia

He enjoyed a huge boost in Germany,
A massive surge in popularity.
His 'empire' now bordered Italy,
With Yugoslavia and Hungary
Also adjacent. It's no mystery
Why Hitler had coveted the country.

---

*I don't write much about my friends, as a rule,
But my senior German teacher, from school,
Was an Austrian, and married to a Jew.
He had taught in Vienna. I never knew,
Until he died (aged over one hundred),
Much about his past. I'd often wondered.
He never spoke of it. From those dark days,
However, here's a story to amaze.
The Principal of the school where he taught
(Classics, I believe) was a wicked sort –
A strong Nazi sympathiser, of course.
Showing not the slightest shred of remorse,
He forced the Herr Doktor to make a choice:
Divorce your wife, or leave. He found his voice.
This honest man turned on his heels and left.
He loved his country and he felt bereft,
But he loved his wife and young son better.
Heeding his conscience to the letter,
He fled to England with his family.
His goodness and courage were plain to see.
It must have been hard. Imagine the pain.
But Austria's loss was Great Britain's gain.

Depression and the Shadow of War

On the threshold now, strategically,
Of most of south-eastern Europe by rail,
By road and river, he could hardly fail.
Had the Führer drawn a line in the sand?
Far from it. Other plans were well in hand.
All eyes were now on the Sudetenland.

Czechoslovakia: independent,
Strongly governed, and a rare testament
To the good sense of those who, in '18,
Carved out that country. Who could have foreseen,
In those far-off days (no one was to blame),
That anyone would dare to make a claim
To those domains where German-speaking folk
Predominated? No word of a joke,
Hitler, posing as a moderate bloke,
Proposed to annex the Sudetenland –
The old Bohemia, you understand
(Or parts of it). Here the majority
(German) were an oppressed minority
In Czechoslovakia as a whole.
Abuse from the Czechs was taking its toll
In a country which (as Hitler would have it),
After Versailles, they'd been forced to inhabit.

All nonsense, of course. These 'Germans', so-called,
Had lived there for centuries. Some, appalled,
Preferred to adhere to the *status quo.*
Others, more cynical, insisted 'no':
Join with the Reich? Why not give it a go?
Most were just happy to go with the flow.

Adolf Hitler, the lowest of the low,
Had no interest, if you want to know,
In the Sudetenland Germans as such.
Their grievances didn't trouble him much.

Rhyming History

His target was the country as a whole.
After Austria he was on a roll,
But Czechoslovakia, at first glance,
Was not so easy. Russia and France
Were Czechoslovakia's staunch allies.
Should Germany spring a nasty surprise,
Hitler could have a lot to answer for.
Nor were his generals ready for war.

Yet he was pushing at an open door.
For Chamberlain, categorically,
Refused to back France in a guarantee
Of Czechoslovakia's security.
He thus bears heavy responsibility
For the future train of sorry events.

Chamberlain thought Hitler was talking sense
When he argued for the protection
Of the Czech Germans. No connexion
Did he make between this position
And the Führer's wider ambition.
Indeed, he harboured no suspicion –
With his head in the sand; he had the knack –
That Germany was planning an attack
On the greater Czechoslovakia.

Sad to say, there was nothing tackier
Than his efforts to override the Czechs.
He reduced their leaders to nervous wrecks,
As they became only too well aware
That Chamberlain refused (or didn't dare)
To stand up to the Germans. Cue: despair.

Such was the background. I'll cut to the chase.
Czechoslovakia should know her place.
This was Chamberlain's message. He lost face,

Depression and the Shadow of War

Among the Czechs, but didn't greatly care.
How they reacted was their own affair.

Chamberlain turns a blind eye

Rather than alienate Germany,
The PM, with a sense of urgency,
Sought to soften up the fickle French. Yet,
Still, Hitler seemed fully intent (you bet)
To go to war for the Sudetenland –
Prior to full invasion, as planned,
One year on, of the rest of the country.
For now, he merely claimed autonomy
For the German-speaking populace. Well,
This still caused ructions, as time would tell.

For the Germans would not be pacified,
And Chamberlain was far from satisfied
When German troop movements, on the border,
Were reported. This was out of order.
The PM's patience was wearing thin.
He sought compromise, but where to begin?
Another note of protest to Berlin?

The wind was taken out of Hitler's sails
When the Czechs (normally as hard as nails)
Consented to local autonomy
For the Sudeten Germans. By golly –
This unexpected change of policy
Threatened to deprive Hitler of his war!

Surprise, surprise – the Führer pressed for more:
The land itself, complete secession
Of the Sudetenland. Obsession,
Mania, madness, call it what you will,
Hitler was adamant. A bitter pill,

Rhyming History

Indeed, for Chamberlain and his cronies –
Lord Halifax, Hoare and other phonies.
Even *The Times* (yes, believe it or not)
Flirted with secession. Tommyrot!
For this, I regret, gave the appearance
Of major government interference.
Halifax was therefore forced to row back
And deny the charge. Onto the attack
Went Hitler: he felt abused and betrayed.
Poor lamb! Chamberlain was duly dismayed.

Europe now teetered on the brink of war.
Churchill was all for laying down the law.
Give ground to Hitler? He'd always want more.
It should be spelt out in clear terms, therefore,
That, should he invade Czech territory,
War would be declared immediately,
With an allied victory to follow.
This was more than Chamberlain could swallow.
Hitler would become ever more reckless
If put to the challenge. Craven, feckless
And naive, Chamberlain ignored Churchill.

He also refused (this a sore point still)
To press the Russians to come on side.
This smacked of political suicide,
In Churchill's view. With the support of France,
And Russia, there was the strongest chance
That Hitler's forces would be driven out,
Should they trigger a war: a complete rout.
For the three allies had serious clout,
And would have triumphed, there seems little doubt,
Had they summoned up the requisite will.
Lacking resolve and political skill,
Chamberlain turned a deaf ear to Churchill.
He ploughed his own furrow, for good or ill.

The Prime Minister visits Herr Hitler

Without informing his closest allies,
The French, Chamberlain sprang a big surprise.
Acting alone, he sent a telegram
To Herr Hitler. He didn't give a damn
For protocol. He would negotiate
With the Führer before it was too late –
Face to face. There was no time to explain
That he'd never been on an aeroplane.

There was little to lose, and much to gain.
This was the finest moment of his life!
Hitler invited him (he brought the wife)
To Berchtesgaten, his mountain retreat.

The amazement in Britain was complete.
This modest and unassuming fella,
With his winged collar and furled umbrella,
Caught the public imagination.
His visit, hailed as a sensation,
Would save Europe. Folk were electrified.
Good old Nev! He was all but deified.

For what? For refusing to draw the line
At flying, at the age of sixty-nine,
For the very first time in his life? Fine,
But there had to be more to it than that.
As for the Führer, I shall eat my hat
If he didn't run rings round the old man.

"*Heil!*" they chorused, as his triumph began,
In the dense forest of Nazi salutes.
Chamberlain's party, in their sombre suits,
Were dwarfed by the Nazi flags. The SS,
Hitler's bodyguard, were dressed to impress.

Chamberlain walks into Hitler's trap

So, Chamberlain met the Führer at last.
The Czechs were appalled, openly aghast:
All their hopes for peace were dwindling fast.
For Hitler was unprepared to bargain.
It soon became clear he cared not a pin
For the wretched Czechs, or for Chamberlain.
The PM hardly knew where to begin.
Adolf Hitler was hell-bent on conquest.
Poor Neville, he could only do his best.
At least he got the Führer to agree
To a diplomatic *fait accompli*
(So he thought). Unless events forced his hand,
Hitler gave Chamberlain to understand

That he would hold fire and not invade.
The worst of compromises had been made,
The honest Czechs browbeaten and betrayed.
But Chamberlain took Hitler at his word.
The Czechs had been spared. Patently absurd.

What exactly had been settled? Who knew?
The Führer (well, this was Chamberlain's view)
Had agreed to respect the Czech frontiers
As they'd stood now for nearly twenty years.
Yet, within Czech borders, the hopes and fears
Of German-speakers had been satisfied.
This 'understanding' would be 'ratified'
As soon as Hitler filled in the detail!
The outcome was perfect. It couldn't fail.

The Prime Minister had fought tooth and nail
For peace. It was sadly to no avail.
For the Führer viewed the situation
Through his own eyes. Self-determination,
For the German Czechs, meant the Czech nation
Would be broken up, in effect destroyed.
Hitler, indeed, got extremely annoyed
When Chamberlain balked at the idea.
The two leaders were poles apart, I fear.
A pathway to peace? Alas, nowhere near.

Another trip to see Hitler

So where was Chamberlain to go from here?
Well, he flew off again, one week later,
For another chat with the dictator –
This on September the 22nd.
The PM, it's generally reckoned,
Was in high spirits. He got a rude shock.
His peace proposals had taken a knock,

Rhyming History

As Hitler changed the goalposts. His demand –
The agenda, it seems, his to command –
Was now for the instant occupation,
Effectively a German invasion,
Of the Sudetenland! The occasion
Was stressful and fraught, the situation
Critical. Chamberlain showed some backbone
(Of sorts). He disapproved of Hitler's tone,
Complained that this was most unexpected,
And that the Führer, whom he'd respected
(Nay, trusted), had failed him. He objected,
In particular, to the timetable,
Pretending, as far as he was able,
That this was a major stumbling block.
As if it all depended on the clock!

Yet when Hitler extended the time frame
(To October the 1st), how in God's name
Did Chamberlain see this 'concession'
As significant? In possession,
Nonetheless, of a raft of promises,
From Hitler, that this ended the business,
And he had no further demands to make
(In Europe or elsewhere), Neville's mistake
Was to take him at his word yet again.

Chamberlain, no doubt, was feeling the strain.
The Czechs, livid at the provocation,
Prepared for full-scale mobilisation.
The threat of a Nazi invasion
Of the Sudetenland, they insisted,
Was an affront, and would be resisted.
The Hitler/Chamberlain 'memorandum',
In effect a final ultimatum,
Was rejected too by the French. Good show.
Even Halifax, a complex fellow,

Was ready to draw a line in the sand
And fly the flag for the Sudetenland.

So, when the Cabinet declared its hand,
Chamberlain submitted. He knew the score.
If Hitler was serious, this meant war.
But what could Britain reasonably do?
The allies were weak. This Chamberlain knew.
Oddly (but known to only a few),
The Germans were weaker! Intriguing stuff,
But had Britain and France called Hitler's bluff,
He might never have got away with it.

Chamberlain refuses to give up

Yet Chamberlain saw little benefit
In giving up his quest for peace. Neville,
A stubborn man, was the very devil.

Determined at all costs to avoid war,
He put pressure on the Czechs to withdraw
Their own forces from the Sudetenland
To make way for Hitler (so underhand),
If the Führer promised not to use force.
The Prime Minister would learn, in due course,
That whatever it was he had to say,
Hitler would have invaded anyway.

How "fantastic" it was, how "horrible,"
Pondered Chamberlain, how "incredible"
That the British were "trying on gas-masks"
And "digging trenches", of all gruesome tasks,
"Because of a quarrel" (some irony,
He inferred) "in a faraway country
"Between people of which we know nothing".
Determined, as ever, to do something,

Rhyming History

Chamberlain offered to fly, yet again,
To meet the Führer. The constant refrain:
Peace at any price – or the transfer
Of Czech territory, if you prefer,
To the aggressor, without recourse
To law, justice or protocol. What sauce.
The offer was craven and misconceived.
Next day, no answer having been received,
Chamberlain rose to address Parliament.
His was a dismal and bitter lament:
German mobilisation, all too soon,
Was set to begin that very afternoon.
War was imminent. He had done all he could.

Chamberlain, nonetheless, was touching wood.
Deladier, for France, and Mussolini
(That other mad dictator), for Italy,
Were both at that very moment, hopefully,
Seeking to persuade Hitler, for Germany,
To come to terms. Britain and France, woefully,
Had sold the Czechs down the river. Nobody,
Listening in the House of Commons that day,
Was prepared for what he was about to say.

Chamberlain was handed a note in mid-flow:
Hitler had agreed to meet him! Would he go?
The PM was hardly a man to say no:
"I need not say what my answer will be!"
The meeting, brokered by Mussolini,
Would take place in Munich the next morning.

Chamberlain the hero

It was as if a new age was dawning.
The Commons went wild, broke into a roar.
The Czechs (who cared?) had been shown the door,
But Europe, pulled back from the brink of war,

Had been saved. "Thank God," one member shouted,
"For the Prime Minister!" No one doubted,
For a moment (well, some cynics, perhaps,
Like Churchill and Eden, difficult chaps),
That this meant peace, a lasting one at that.

Munich

At Munich the Führer, the little rat,
Had it all sewn up. He made no pretence
That the Czechs, distinguished by their absence,
Had any say in the matter at all.
Chamberlain was expected to play ball.
This he did. Hitler put him at his ease
With friendly words, but refused, if you please,
To "waste time" on "such trivialities"
As compensation for property lost.
The allies caved in, at a horrible cost.

So the Sudetenland was surrendered.
Czechoslovakia was dismembered,
Her northern frontiers now occupied
By the Germans, her borders open wide,
And her rail communications cut.
A free Czech nation? Anything but.
800,000 Czechs (who said sorry?)
Comprised a new oppressed minority
Within the Sudetenland. Like it or not,
Hitler, who never fired a single shot,
Had been handed his winnings on a plate.

A bleak future of tyranny and hate
Was the lot of those Germans who opposed
The Nazis – more folk than often supposed:
A tale of torture, misery and woe
Under the heel of Hitler's Gestapo.

Rhyming History

Prime Minister Chamberlain was well pleased.
War had been averted, Hitler appeased,
Britain saved from disaster. Neville knew,
However, that there was more he could do.
He would make the whole of Europe secure
From the grim prospect of another war.

He pressed for another meeting, therefore,
With Herr Hitler. Chamberlain took a walk
To the Führer's flat. There they had a talk.
He took out of his pocket, pre-prepared,
A paper (two typed copies). How he dared,
I have no idea. But he was spared
Any awkwardness or embarrassment.
For Hitler was bullish, and quite content
To consider the proffered document.

Re. the agreement signed the night before,
That was symbolic of the new *rapport*
Between the two nations. Furthermore,
They now agreed "never to go to war
"With one another again". Problem solved!
For both parties professed themselves "resolved"
That "the method of consultation"
Should be the one means, for each nation,
By which any questions of concern
Might be considered. Would he never learn?

Hitler signed for Chamberlain's benefit.
He never meant a single word of it.

The statement was the icing on the cake
For the Prime Minister, make no mistake.
He knew that Munich would be make or break
And he came home in triumph. "I've got it!"
He declared, as he drew from his pocket
The signed paper, the offending docket.

"Peace with honour"

From the first-floor window in Downing Street
He waved to the crowds, his mission complete.
"This," he proclaimed, with undisguised glee,
"Is the second time* in our history
"That there has come back from Germany…

---

*The first occasion, apparently,
Was when Prime Minister Disraeli
Returned home in 1878,
Following the Congress of Berlin. Fate,
It seems, dealt rather more fairly with him.
The comparison was signally dim.

Rhyming History

"Peace with honour." It's unclear, to me,
How this was the second time. So be it.

But his hollow success, as I see it,
Was a sorry affair. He concluded:
"I believe" (was ever one so deluded?)
"It is peace for our time." Game, set and match
To the Prime Minister. So, where was the catch?

Few seemed to spot one, if the truth be told.
His cheering fans were a sight to behold,
As the PM, on his way to the King,
Drove down the Mall. The scene was amazing:
An eager sea of people, flag-waving,
Jumping on the running board of his car...
Man of the moment! A popular star!

Congratulatory letters galore
Poured in to Number Ten. Gifts by the score:
Fine wines and fishing rods, watches and more.
One of the hundreds of compliments paid
Was from the Chamberlains' own kitchen maid –
Nothing too effusive, you understand,
Just a simple note in her clear, round hand.

Attlee's criticism

There followed speech after speech of high praise
In the House of Commons. Those were the days!
But Attlee, for Labour, the little louse,
Condemned Munich and divided the House.
A most "bitter humiliation,"
He called it. The gallant Czech nation
Had been "handed over to a ruthless
"Despotism". The patent truth of this
Could not be denied. Attlee was all gloom.

Churchill lambasts the Prime Minister

Churchill, in a stirring speech, foretold doom.
Forty-five minutes he was on his feet.
"A total, unmitigated defeat"
We had sustained. Hitler showed no remorse.
The "victuals" had been served up "course by course".
Instead of being "snatched from the table" –
Assuming the Germans had been able –
The Prime Minister's "intense exertions"
Had delivered them! Of all assertions,
This must surely have been the most bitter.

Winston Churchill, ever the big hitter,
Described the Czech state as "silent, mournful"
And "broken". Not only was he scornful,
He uttered this provoking prophecy:
Now, "as an independent entity",
The country could no longer be "maintained".
The time-scale might be measured, he explained,
By years – or even by months, Churchill feared.

It's uncanny, more than a little weird,
How accurate he was. An awful dream,
But he foresaw that the Nazi *régime*
Would engulf the country and he was right.

When it occurred, it happened overnight.
March the 15th, '39, was the date
When the rest of the Czechoslovak state
Fell to the Nazis, a terrible fate.

Churchill's dire warnings, pity to relate,
Cut little ice with Chamberlain. Sadly,
There was a risk he might suffer badly
Down in his Epping constituency.

Had he been 'de-selected', imagine!
As successor to Neville Chamberlain,
Forget it. The Tory 'young Turks' – Eden
(Ex-Foreign Secretary), Macmillan,
Duncan Sandys, Richard Law and Bob Boothby –
Abstained in the vote. Somewhat ruefully,
They failed to vote against the government,
But made no secret of their discontent.
Duff Cooper, the Admiralty's First Lord,
Resigned, although he too could ill afford
To cast his vote to unseat Chamberlain.
The Tories had a comfortable win.

One point that Winston Churchill also made
Was that democracy had been betrayed
By Nazi power. Happy to profess
A friendship with the German people, yes;
But the onward course of barbarism,
Symbolised by poisonous Nazism,
Which "vaunts the spirit of aggression
"And conquest", spelt anarchy, oppression
And tyranny. It was useless to pretend
That Britain could ever be a trusted friend
To the Nazis. "Pitiless brutality",
The "murderous force" of Hitler's Germany,
Was alien to British democracy.

Kristallnacht

Churchill was vindicated, more's the pity,
When Jewish shops, on the 10th of November,
Were smashed and looted. German Jews, remember,
Had been harassed and subject to abuse,
For years, under Hitler. A new excuse,
However, he now found. This was obscene.
A Polish Jewish youth, aged seventeen,

Killed a junior German diplomat,
In Paris, as a sort of tit-for-tat –
Not that I make any excuse for that –
For the expulsion, from Germany,
Of 20,000 Polish Jews. To me,
It smacked of hideous hypocrisy
To seek 'revenge'. That was Hitler, you see:
Prepared for any opportunity
To present himself as fighting the fight
For all decent Germans. So, overnight,
Not only were synagogues set alight,
But shop windows smashed and Jews assaulted –
Nay, murdered. The plan could not be 'faulted',
The terror executed to a T.

Moreover, the Jewish community
Was subject to a huge collective fine,
Levied by the perpetrators, the swine
(The Nazis), to make good the damage done!
This, to them, was a harmless bit of fun.

The outrage was followed by a decree
That Jews should cease trading (yes, really)
By the end of the year: no business,
No work... Could it get any worse than this?

Kristallnacht this dreadful event was called.
All good people in Britain stood appalled,
Chamberlain included. Yes, "horrified"
Was Neville. Yet he remained dewy-eyed
When it came to Hitler. Another year
Of appeasement was on the cards, I fear.

Chamberlain's paranoia

Chamberlain became increasingly annoyed
With his critics. He would become paranoid
At the slightest whiff of opposition.
This gravely undermined the position
Of the sceptics, men of manifest goodwill.

The PM finally went in for the kill,
By closing down (a major travesty, this)
The News Department at the Foreign Office.

This had been largely staffed, Chamberlain reckoned,
By anti-appeasers. Not for a second
Did he consider that alternative views
Were healthy. The sole source of government news,
Believe it or not, was now 10 Downing Street:
Anything to keep the Prime Minister sweet.

Rearmament was still very small beer.
One thing calculated to raise a cheer,
Post-Munich, was that spending on defence
Was set to increase. This of course made sense.
Chamberlain was loth to antagonise
Hitler, but considered it only wise
To balance efforts at diplomacy
With strategic strength. His hesitancy,
However, to rearm on a large scale
Was opposed (some surprise, this) tooth and nail
By the Foreign Secretary, no less,
Lord Halifax. It was rather a mess,
Quite frankly, but Halifax did his best.

It was also in Britain's interest,
His Lordship had the wisdom to suggest,
To broaden the base of the government.
Bring in Labour, that's what Halifax meant,
Figures such as Morrison and Attlee.
'Know-it-all' Neville would never agree.

He also rejected, predictably,
A plan to bring Anthony Eden back –
The man he had once been tempted to sack.

Rearmament

Yet rearmament did proceed apace.
In October '38 (a disgrace)
The Army had only two divisions
Fully equipped. So some hard decisions,
Not before time, had now to be taken
To build its strength. If I'm not mistaken,
There were still, by September '39,
Just five units. Even as a baseline
This was inadequate, as time would prove.

Investment in the Royal Air Force

The Royal Air Force, though, was on the move.
Government planners were quick to approve
A new line in bombers: the Wellington,
Hampton and Blenheim; and the Hurricane
And Spitfire fighters. Both these were tested
(The latter) when Britain's future rested,
Precariously, on the RAF.
No longer a dialogue of the deaf,
The ease with which the aircraft industry
Worked in tandem with the Air Ministry
Had truly to be seen to be believed.
The rate at which new targets were achieved
Was phenomenal: plans, over two years,
For some 12,000 aircraft. It appears,
Moreover, this figure was exceeded
By more than half. Chamberlain succeeded,
For once, in keeping his critics at bay.
The PM was confident. Chocks away!

The Royal Navy ignored

The Royal Navy was unaffected
By Munich. Its budgets were respected,
But not increased. This was unexpected,
For naval superiority
Over Germany (with Italy)
Was at risk. More cash, more's the pity,
For the RAF passed the Navy by –
A slap in the face, no word of a lie.

Yet by '38, I have to confess,
Spending on armaments was still far less
In Britain than it was in Germany.
The proportion, almost certainly,

Of Germany's national income
Spent on arms (a considerable sum)
Was an astounding twenty-five *per cent*,
Compared to Britain, where the money spent
Was under nine *per cent* (seven or eight).
Since 1934 the spending rate
In Germany (this barely seems decent)
Had risen by some five hundred *per cent*,
While in Britain, from a far lower base,
The growth was half that. A further disgrace.

One advance to be proud of, in the air,
Was radar. Baldwin had been in despair.
"The bomber," he said, "will always get through."
His colleagues agreed, but what could they do?

Hideous numbers of casualties
Were predicted – millions, if you please,
Mainly civilians in the cities –
Should war be declared. Figures such as these
Were unthinkable. The only defence
Was the bomber. This, of course, was nonsense.
The bomber was an engine of offence,
Well capable of destroying cities,
But saving them? No! A thousand pities.

Radar

There was no adequate form of defence
Against aerial bombing. No pretence,
Indeed, was ever made to this effect.
It was a scientist, as you'd expect,
Who saved the day. Prepare to genuflect
(Down on one knee) to Robert Watson-Watt,
Inventor of radar. A cheerful Scot,
He saved our bacon. We owe him a lot.

Watt started as a meteorologist,
Whose detailed study of the atmospherics
Emitted by thunderstorms enabled him
To issue warnings to airmen. On a whim,
He exploited his knowledge of radio
To locate new hazards. Those in the know
Were well impressed. This laddie would go far.

Those first steps were the genesis of radar,
By which radio instruments could detect
Distant objects in the air. Please don't expect
A full scientific explanation,
But radar proved to be a sensation.
Developed over four years from '35,
Watt's invention was ready to 'go live'
By 1939, a nasty surprise
For the Germans. For now the coveted prize
Of aerial defence was well within sight.
Radar stations stretched from the Isle of Wight

As far north as the Orkneys. Air warfare
Had been revolutionised. Hardly fair,
Perhaps, on the Germans, who had no radar –
But we had the wherewithal, so there you are.
Enemy bombers could no longer surprise
Our forces. Fighters now had time to rise
To the challenge. The fortunes of 'the few'
Depended on radar, and this they knew.
Many planes got through, of course, those who dared,
But hundreds of thousands of lives were spared.

ARP

Following Munich, it made complete sense
To beef up the country's civil defence.
Air Raid Precautions (the 'ARP')
Performed a vital role. Their work was key,
Were Britain, on the home front, to survive.

When, in the early days of '35,
The ARP came into existence,
The people were asked to give assistance,
As volunteers. Local authorities
Were to shoulder responsibilities
For protecting their citizens. Duties
Were imposed on these regional bodies
With respect to training and discipline.

Thousands were recruited (men, few women)
As Air Raid Wardens. With a war to win,
Doctors and general medical staff
Signed up. It was all a bit of a laugh,
Perhaps, at first. But in the darker days,
As the war entered its more deadly phase,
The courage of these countless volunteers
Has the power, still, to move one to tears.

Anderson shelters and evacuation plans

A man of massive popular appeal,
Sir John Anderson, the Lord Privy Seal,
Was promoted from the Civil Service
To the Cabinet. Sir John deserved this.
The top administrator of the age,
He was planner, boffin, government sage
And general all-round egg-head in one.
He did his best to see the war was won,
At home. The challenge was clear and real.
400,000 shelters, made of steel,
Were provided for use by families
With gardens. For larger communities,
Provision for shelter was also made.
Plans for evacuation were laid
For mothers with small children, and the sick.
This was sensible and realistic.
Who wanted to end up a statistic?
The danger was pressing and time was short.
The plans enjoyed broad popular support.

Sir John Anderson was forthright and bold.
The ARP budget increased fourfold –
To fifty-five million, we are told.
Issued to every British household
Was the *Guide to National Service*.
In advance of the oncoming crisis,
Everyone was urged to volunteer.
The time was ripe and the message was clear:
Everybody had a part to play.

Appeasement continues

Had appeasement policy had its day?
Most certainly not! It still had a place.
Chamberlain, determined not to lose face,

Trundled on. For here was Mussolini,
Making warlike noises in Italy,
Staking a claim to Corsica, Tunis
And Nice from the French. Complete nonsense, this,
But he had watched Hitler's annexation
Of Austria with envy. 'Vexation'
Might have been Mussolini's middle name.
A disgusting character, he sought fame
Through conquest. Remember, if you will,
Abyssinia, a nightmare still.

Chamberlain resolved, for good or ill,
To visit Mussolini. A *tête-à-tête*
Could do the trick. Appeasement? Not dead quite yet.
Relations with Hitler, never easy,
Would improve with the help of Mussolini.

A toast to Italy's King

So, in January, 1939,   **1939**
He set off with Halifax. A hand-shake? Fine.
For Chamberlain, yet again, made no pretence
Of his motive: simply not give offence –
To anybody! What sticks in the throat most
Was Britain's Prime Minister drinking a toast,
At a banquet, to Victor Emmanuel,
As Emperor of Abyssinia. Well,
That took the biscuit. Yet Chamberlain, the dope,
Travelled back from Italy with renewed hope.
He had found Mussolini quite "straightforward"
And "considerate". If peace was his reward,
His visit would have been worthwhile. A fascist?
Who cared? Another he added to his list
(Of new friends) was General Franco of Spain.
Chamberlain reckoned there was little to gain
From withholding British recognition
Of Franco's 'government'. His position

Was this: as a possible friend and ally
Of Germany, the General, by and by,
Could be useful to Britain. Pie in the sky,
Of course, but Chamberlain thought it worth a try.

The General, anyway (no doubt of it),
Had the gumption to keep well out of it.
On the 22nd of May, Germany
Announced a new alliance with Italy,
Hardly a surprise: a 'Pact of Steel', so-called.
Britain and her allies were duly appalled.

The fall of Czechoslovakia

For the Czechoslovak 'rump', crisis loomed.
Hitler seized his chance. The country was doomed.
There were many who cried, "I told you so!" –
But this was a veritable death-blow
To Chamberlain's hopes. The Nazis swept in
On the 15th of March, an easy 'win'.

The nation had earlier been split
(The Sudetenland apart), with one bit,
Slovakia, under the 'tutelage'
Of Hitler (a dubious privilege),
Already proclaiming 'independence'.
This was window-dressing, utter nonsense.
The residual Czechs made no pretence
Of their iron determination
To remain a separate nation.

Adolf Hitler, a man on a mission,
Bullied the poor Czechs into submission.
He summoned their President to Berlin
And forced him to sign up to the ruin
Of his sad country. A very sick man,
President Hácha 'agreed' to the plan,

And by 9 a.m. the very same day
The Germans had occupied Prague. Some say
That Europe need never have gone to war –
And this has been said many times before –
Had Hitler's army been stopped in its tracks.

Certainly the likes of Lord Halifax,
And Neville Chamberlain, would not have dared.
While Churchill and his supporters despaired,
Czechoslovakia fell. Yet again,
No shots were heard. But Europe felt the pain.

All Chamberlain's best hopes were at an end.
How could the PM possibly pretend,
When Hitler's forces were on the attack,
That the Germans were only claiming back
Territory denied them by Versailles?
It was now impossible to deny
His expansionist ambitions.
In the most hopeless of positions,
Chamberlain's policy was in tatters.

Poland next?

Yet these were the weightiest of matters.
With the Czech state now annexed to the Reich,
What would Hitler do next? Where would he strike?
Chamberlain, following where Churchill led,
Turned his foreign policy on its head.
Suddenly Poland was in the spotlight.
There were rumours (which turned out to be right)
That Hitler was casting his evil eye
On the Poles. Chamberlain (now 'do or die')
Upped the ante. Before it was too late,
The Führer's endeavour to "dominate
"The world by force," the PM insisted,
Was a challenge that should be resisted.

The Russians proposed a conference
To consider the issue. This made sense.
But the Russian initiative
Threw Chamberlain onto the defensive.

He distrusted the Russians. The Poles,
Moreover, the poor unfortunate souls,
Had suffered most terribly in the past
At Russia's hands. Churchill was aghast
(And others) when Chamberlain turned his back
On the Soviets. Neville had the knack,
It seems, of blundering down the wrong track,
Just as a golden opportunity
Presented itself. Then, quite suddenly,
He offered (with France, bilaterally)
The following cast-iron guarantee
To Poland: "all support in their power...
"His Majesty's Government" (come the hour)
"Would lend the Polish government". Never,
In Great Britain's long history, ever,

Had such a peacetime alliance been made
With eastern Europeans. Unafraid,
However, brazen, and at full throttle,
Chamberlain at least displayed some bottle.

Czechoslovakia had passed him by,
But the more distant country (why, oh why?)
Was offered protection. Worth a try?
Well, perhaps. But Britain was quite unfit
To act! Lloyd George put his finger on it,
In the Commons, the old rapscallion:
"You could not send a single battalion
"To Poland... if war occurred tomorrow."
He spoke less in anger than in sorrow.
But when the time did come, the Welsh Wizard
Was proved correct. It sticks in the gizzard,
But the British offered no help at all.
When the Poles had their backs against the wall,
They received no military support –
No arms, no men... nothing of any sort.

What did he think this was? Some kind of sport?
Weasel words, empty promises, a disgrace...
The whole affair blew up in Chamberlain's face.

Hitler had set his sights, more's the pity,
On Danzig, which became a 'Free City'
Under the terms of Versailles. Germany
Now demanded its return. Furthermore,
The issue of the 'Polish Corridor',
So-called, Poland's path to the Baltic Sea,
Which separated greater Germany
From East Prussia, had to be resolved.
Limit access for the Poles! Problem solved!
Talks with Russia finally started,
But these, at very best, were half-hearted

And tentative. Stalin was unimpressed.
Chamberlain, less than his pitiful best,
Was all of a-dither. "Profound distrust"
He professed of Russia. Dry as dust,
He even refused to fly to Moscow
To meet 'Uncle Joe'. Now, as insults go,
This was a corker. Three times he had flown
To see Hitler, which Stalin must have known.

The Nazi-Soviet Pact

His expectations were overblown.
He imagined Stalin would fall in line
And support the Poles. It suited him fine
To wait on events. So it came as a shock,
And his credit abroad took another knock,

Depression and the Shadow of War

When Hitler and Stalin, out of the blue,
Signed a Nazi-Soviet pact: a *coup*
For Germany; for Poland, disaster.
Catastrophe beckoned. Ever faster,
The momentum was building towards war.
For Germany had managed to secure
Russian neutrality. For his part,
Stalin won a promise (not a bad start),
An assurance from Hitler to limit
His gains in Poland. Shocking, isn't it,
To watch them carving up and sharing out
The spoils. Wicked, no shadow of a doubt.

Hitler kept the German people on side.
Nazi propaganda intensified,
As reports of Polish oppression
Created a quite false impression
That ethnic Germans living in Poland –
Some 800,000, you understand –
Had suffered widespread abuse and hatred.
This was stirred up, you can take it as read,
By the Nazis, to add to Poland's plight.

Convinced that the British would never fight,
Hitler prepared. The Führer was half right:
Chamberlain, until the stroke of midnight,
Would always prefer to negotiate.
If offered the choice, he would sit and wait.
He pressurised the Poles (heard this before?)
To opt for anything rather than war.
Could they not yield a bit over Danzig?
Chamberlain, in truth, didn't care a fig
For Poland. Cornered into 'thinking big',
The PM found he had nowhere to turn.
Hitler meant business. Would he never learn?
The Poles, in any case, were adamant:
No surrender – a glowing testament

Rhyming History

To their huge courage and integrity.
Chamberlain still swithered, more's the pity.
The PM, a veteran appeaser,
Still relished his role as a crowd pleaser.
Hitler could be persuaded. All was not lost.
War must be avoided, whatever the cost.

Hitler invades Poland

But there was no holding the Germans back.
The Führer gave the order to attack
On August the 31st. The PM
Was appalled. At 4.45 a.m.,
On September the 1st, Hitler's forces
Crossed the Polish border – tanks (and horses*),
For this was modern warfare, not a game.
Would there be war? Not in Chamberlain's name.
It appears he favoured a conference!
Needless to say, this was utter nonsense.

---

*Relatively short of oil resources
For most of the war, the Germans used horses,
In massive numbers, for transportation
Of troops and artillery. Frustration,
Caused by the lack of mechanisation,
Was relieved, by way of compensation,
By the horse. Germany entered World War Two
With some half a million horses. Mules, too,
Were used for heavier, more mundane duties.
Two and a half million beasts, the beauties,
Served the Nazis. Many ended up as meat,
Sadly, when the troops ran out of things to eat.
On the whole I like to keep my footnotes sweet,
But these are the facts, unvarnished and complete.

Depression and the Shadow of War

The Prime Minister hesitates

The Germans had already bombed Warsaw.
If that didn't count as an act of war,
What would? The same day, in the evening,
Chamberlain sent the Germans a 'warning' –
Not to be seen as an ultimatum –
To withdraw their troops. It was clear, to some,
That the Prime Minister would never act.

In the Commons, the PM was attacked
From all sides. The 2nd of September:
In a debate folk would long remember,
Chamberlain would still not talk of war.
If German forces agreed to withdraw
('Agreed', mark you: they didn't have to leave,
Not yet), then the British, can you believe,
Would overlook all that had taken place
And open talks. Anything to save face.

The Commons in revolt

The Prime Minister sat down to silence.
Never in the Commons, before or since,
Has a more cowardly statement been heard.
His proposal was patently absurd.
Chamberlain's embarrassment was complete
When the Labour leader rose to his feet –
Acting leader, rather: Arthur Greenwood –
And articulated, as best he could,
The mood of the House. It was a Tory,
Leo Amery, who made history:
"Speak for England, Arthur," Amery cried!
The House of Commons was electrified.
"Every minute's delay," said Greenwood,
"Now means the loss of life." Arthur came good.

Our "national honour" was at stake.
Greenwood had touched a nerve, make no mistake.
In private, he gave Chamberlain warning.
War had to be declared the next morning,
Else "it would be impossible to hold
"The House". This was more than a little bold,
But the Prime Minister had to be told.

Most of Chamberlain's ministers agreed.
Sir John Simon (Chancellor) took the lead.
In Cabinet, at eleven that night,
The beleaguered PM got quite a fright,
When a group of his colleagues refused to budge
Until he came to his senses. No more fudge.
How much longer did the Poles have to wait?
"How long are we prepared to vacillate?" –
Greenwood had asked earlier. Chamberlain
Knew his number was up. He could not win.
He had no option but to agree.

The British ultimatum

Next morning, at 9 a.m. precisely,
Great Britain delivered to Germany
Her ultimatum. It caused some surprise
In Berlin, where they'd been slow to surmise
That Britain would ever come to the aid
Of the Poles. They were deceived, I'm afraid.

War with Germany

The British ultimatum expired
At 11 a.m. Bitter, tired,
A near-broken man, Chamberlain broadcast
To the people. We were at war at last.
His tone was pitiful, grim and downcast,

Depression and the Shadow of War

"But I am confident that right will prevail".
He faced a challenge on a massive scale.
Regrets and heartache were to no avail.

Britain led, with France six hours behind,
But in truth both countries were flying blind.
Neither proud nation, I think you'll find,
Lifted a finger to defend Poland.

The distant Dominions, New Zealand
And Australia, followed the British.
Their gallant troops would fight to the finish.
The Kiwis and the Aussies jumped straight in,
A vote of confidence in Chamberlain.
They did not consult their Parliaments,
Unlike the more cautious governments
Of both Canada and South Africa.
The latter country, in particular,
Appeared less than keen. Her Prime Minister
Preferred to stay neutral, no ifs, no buts,
But Herzog was replaced by J. C. Smuts –
Then her Parliament voted for war.*

India (as had been the case before,
In 1914, according to law)
Signed up, as did the other colonies.
Had they sought to offer 'apologies',
They would have been overruled. Autocratic?
Yes! But their commitment was automatic.

---

*Eire, under Eamon de Valera,
Declared herself a neutral area
And kept well out of the war from day one.
She had no wish to tangle with the Hun.

Poland's fate

Sadly, for Poland, this all came too late.
The Poles were abandoned, left to their fate.
Danzig suffered early sustained attack
From the sea. The invaders were held back,
Briefly, as brave Polish volunteers
Fought for the city. It ended in tears.
The few survivors were executed,
As Danzig ('free' no longer) was looted
And abused. Leading citizens – teachers,
Politicians, scientists, preachers –
Were rounded up. For the Nazis were scared
Of future resistance. They'd come prepared.
Those who defied their orders, those who dared,
Were shot. The Jews were a target, of course,
As the city succumbed to brute force.

A huge German army crossed the border,
Causing widespread terror and disorder.
From the west they came, Pomerania
And Silesia; from Slovakia,
Down in the south; and from East Prussia,
In the north. Oddly enough, Russia,
For now, was of no special concern –
Though the poor beleaguered Poles would soon learn.

They got a bloody nose, to be exact.
They had no knowledge of the secret pact
Between Molotov and Ribbentrop. No:
They thought their eastern borders were safe. So,
All their resources they concentrated
Against the Germans. They'd hesitated,
Briefly, when Britain and France warned Warsaw
That the Poles themselves could trigger the war,
Should the Germans see them mobilising.

Depression and the Shadow of War

I confess to finding it surprising
That they swallowed this. Be that as it may,
The small matter of a few days' delay
Would have made no difference anyway.

All that is matter for another day.
For now, I regret, suffice it to say
The Second World War was under way.

Bibliography

Paul Addison, *The Road to 1945* (Jonathan Cape, 1975)

Jonathan Bastable, *Prime Ministers – Amazing and Extraordinary Facts* (David and Charles, 2011)

Stephen Bates, *Asquith* (Haus Publishing Limited, 2006)

David Cannadine, *George V* (Penguin Books, 2014)

Terry Coleman, *The Old Vic* (Faber & Faber Ltd., 2014)

Max Egremont, *Balfour* (Phoenix, 1998)

Bryan Forbes, *That Despicable Race – A History of the British Acting Tradition* (Elm Tree Books, 1980)

E. H. H. Green, *Balfour* (Haus Publishing Limited, 2006)

Roy Hattersley, *David Lloyd George, The Great Outsider* (Abacus, 2012)

Roy Jenkins, *Asquith* (Collins, 1964)

Denis Judd, *The Life and Times of George V* (Weidenfeld & Nicolson, with Book Club Associates, 1973)

Graham Macklin, *Chamberlain* (Haus Publishing, 2006)

David Marquand, *Britain since 1918 – The Strange Case of British Democracy* (Weidenfeld & Nicolson, 2008)

David Marquand, *Ramsay MacDonald* (Jonathan Cape Ltd., 1977)

Fiona McDonald, *Britain in the 1920s* (Pen & Sword History, 2020)

Keith Middlemas, *The Life and Times of George VI* (Weidenfeld & Nicolson, with Book Club Associates, 1973)

Kenneth O. Morgan, *The Age of Lloyd George – The Liberal Party and British Politics, 1890-1929* (George Allen and Unwin Ltd., 1971)

Kenneth O. Morgan, *The Twentieth Century (1914-2000)* (in *The Oxford History of Britain,* ed. Kenneth O. Morgan – Oxford University Press, 2001)

Kevin Morgan, *Ramsay MacDonald* (Haus Publishing Limited, 2006)

Charles Loch Mowat, *Britain between the Wars, 1918-1940* (Methuen & Co. Ltd., 1955)

Matthew Parris (with Jude Kelly), *Great Lives: Lilian Baylis* (BBC, Radio 4)

Matthew Parris (with A. A. Gill and Elizabeth Shafer), *Great Lives: Arthur Neville Chamberlain* (BBC, Radio 4)

Anne Perkins, *Baldwin* (Haus Publishing Limited, 2006)

J. B. Priestley, *English Journey* (William Heinemann, 1934)

Martin Pugh, *We Danced All Night – A Social History of Britain between the Wars* (Vintage Books, 2009)

Hugh Purcell, *Lloyd George* (Haus Publishing Limited, 2006)

A. J. P. Taylor, *English History, 1914-1945* (Oxford University Press, 1965)

Andrew Taylor, *Bonar Law* (Haus Publishing Limited, 2006)

G. M. Trevelyan, *A Shortened History of England* (Penguin, 1959)

RHYMING HISTORY
The Story of England in Verse

EARLIER VOLUMES IN THE SERIES

Volume One: 55BC – 1485
THE ROMANS TO THE WARS OF THE ROSES

An entertaining, ironic and accessible journey through our history from the first arrival of Julius Caesar in 55BC to the defeat of Richard the Third at Bosworth Field in 1485.

An ebook of Volume One and a CD of excerpts are also available.

Volume Two: 1485 – 1603
THE TUDORS

From Henry the Seventh to Queen Elizabeth, this volume spans one of the most exciting, turbulent and colourful periods of English history.

Volume Three: 1603 – 1649
THE EARLY STUARTS AND CIVIL WAR

Where James the First was intelligent and astute, his son was obstinate and rash. Charles the First plunged his kingdom into bloody civil war.

Volume Four: 1649 – 1660
CROMWELL AND THE COMMONWEALTH

This volume charts the early success and final decline of the new Commonwealth, closing with the triumphant return of Charles the Second to reclaim his lost kingdom.

Volume Five: 1660 – 1685
CHARLES THE SECOND AND THE RESTORATION

The Restoration of Charles the Second ushered in a new age of scandal, danger and political turmoil. The cast of characters is rich and diverse.

Volume Six: 1685 – 1688
JAMES THE SECOND, THE FORGOTTEN KING

James the Second was headstrong, vain and inept. He inherited a kingdom at peace, but rebellion was in the air. The Glorious Revolution was about to begin.

Volume Seven: 1688 – 1714
GLORIOUS REVOLUTION,
THE LAST OF THE STUARTS

In the Glorious Revolution, King William and Queen Mary were invited to reign jointly. When Queen Anne died childless, the Stuart dynasty drew to a close.

Volume Eight: 1714 – 1760
THE EARLY HANOVERIANS

The accession of George the First ushered in an era of change. The turbulent reign of George the Second ended with the celebrated Year of Victories.

Volume Nine: 1760 – 1789
GEORGE THE THIRD AND THE LOSS OF AMERICA

The reign of 'Farmer George' was the third longest in British history, but the first signs of the King's madness were beginning to show.

Volume Ten: 1789 – 1837
THE LAST OF THE HANOVERIANS

These were momentous times: the rise of Napoleon, the Great Reform Act and the abolition of the slave trade. With the death of William the Fourth, the Hanoverian era was at an end.

Volume Eleven: 1837 – 1858
THE EARLY VICTORIANS

The Victorian Age was one of vision, enterprise and conflict. The Great Exhibition heralded a time of progress and invention, but the Crimean War and the Indian Mutiny were soon to cast long shadows.

Volume Twelve: 1858 – 1901
THE LATER VICTORIANS

The death of Prince Albert left Victoria bereft. This was a great age of achievement, dominated by political rivals Gladstone and Disraeli. The Queen's final days were overshadowed by the Boer War.

Volume Thirteen: 1901 – 1922
THE EDWARDIANS AND THE GREAT WAR

This was the age of Asquith and Lloyd George, Britain's two Prime Ministers during the Great War. This terrible conflict tore Europe apart. The Treaty of Versailles solved nothing.

TO BE PUBLISHED IN 2023

Volume Fifteen: 1939 – 1945
THE SECOND WORLD WAR

A mere twenty years after the Treaty of Versailles the world was again at war. This volume covers the six years of this dreadful conflict, at home and abroad.

Please visit our website for excerpts from all these volumes and for news of performances of the verse.

www.rhyminghistory.co.uk